Steven Croft

ESSENTIALS

Year 9
KS3 English
Coursebook

How to Use this Coursebook

A Note to the Teacher

This coursebook covers the requirements of the Level 1 Functional Skills for English appropriate to Year 9. Guidance and practice material relating to these skills is integrated into the main content of the book to reflect the structure of the new Programme of Study.

This is the third of three English coursebooks for students at KS3. Each coursebook comprises...
- clear, concise content appropriate to that year
- questions and tasks to reinforce students' learning and help improve their confidence.

This coursebook is split into 12 topics. The first pages of a topic contain the content. They feature...
- **key words** picked out in colour in the text and listed in a box at the end of each topic
- a **Quick Test** to test understanding.

The final three pages in a topic contain questions and exercises to provide skills practice and reinforce students' understanding:
- **Key Words Exercise** – requires students to understand the definitions of key words.
- **Testing Understanding** – comprises a literacy exercise.
- **Skills Practice** – devoted to a relevant task to develop the students' English skills.

A pull-out answer book is included in the centre of this book. It contains the answers to the questions in the Quick Tests and to the practice sections of this coursebook.

Each coursebook is supported by a workbook for further practice and learning.

A Note to the Student

We're sure you'll enjoy using this coursebook, but follow these helpful hints to make the most of it:
- Make sure you understand the key words before moving on. These words include technical terms that you should be able to understand and use correctly, plus words that will help to expand and develop your vocabulary. If you don't understand them, look back at the context in which they're used to gain a sense of their meaning, ask your teacher or use a dictionary.
- Try to write in Standard English, use correct punctuation and good sentence construction. Read back what you have written to make sure it makes sense. Some questions require extra research, using dictionaries, encyclopedias and thesauruses, or the Internet.

- The tick boxes on the Contents page let you track your progress: put a tick in each box when you're confident that you know the topic.
- The questions marked with a light bulb symbol ( ) are included to help you focus on different aspects of the text. No answers are included. Instead, we suggest you write down your answers and discuss your ideas in pairs, in a small group or with your teacher.
- For many of the skills practice and extension questions, there is no right or wrong answer. Once you have your answer, refer back to the original question and make sure you have covered all the points, then ask a classmate or teacher to read your answer. Ask them questions to find out if you have communicated your ideas effectively.

Contents

Descriptive Writing

What is Covered in this Topic?

This topic looks at...
- using description to create setting, atmosphere or mood
- using description to help develop characters.

Descriptive Writing

The purpose of descriptive writing is always the same – to create a picture in words of whatever you're describing so that you give your reader a vivid impression of the place, event, **characters**, etc.

Descriptive writing can be used in two main ways, both in imaginative and non-fiction writing:

1. It can be used as the main focus of a piece of writing, e.g. if you're writing a **description** of a place you visited on holiday or describing something that has happened to you.
2. It can be used to make a particular part of a piece of writing more vivid, e.g. to give a detailed impression of a character or scene.

Effective Description

An effective description should...
- capture and hold the reader's attention
- be **convincing**, whether it's based on reality or made up out of your imagination
- be based on **observation**
- use **language** effectively.

Choosing your Words

To make your description effective it's really important to choose your words carefully. Remember that words don't just have a specific meaning; they can also suggest different kinds of feelings and emotions.

For example, 'frightened' and 'terrified' both have the same basic meaning, but the feelings or impressions they give aren't quite the same.

💡 *What do you think the difference is between 'frightened' and 'terrified'?*

You might feel that 'terrified' suggests a stronger, more intense kind of fear than the word 'frightened'.

To help you pick the right word to convey the meaning you want, you might find a thesaurus useful (this is a book that gives you lots of alternative words to describe a particular meaning).

Making your Description Vivid

There are various techniques you can use to make your descriptions more vivid and original so that you capture your reader's interest and give them a really good sense of what you're describing.

Here are some ideas:
- Use various senses to create a strong impression – lots of descriptions focus on what can be seen, but don't forget that touch, taste, sound and smell can add vivid details to description too.
- Use adverbs (words that describe verbs) to add to the description of actions.
- Use adjectives (words that describe nouns) to make a real difference to the vividness of the description.

- Use similes (which compare one thing to another), metaphors (which say that one thing *is* another), and onomatopoeia (words that sound like the sound they're describing, e.g. bang, crash).
- Use a varied vocabulary (here's where your thesaurus can help – a good dictionary is very useful too to check the meanings of words you find in your thesaurus).
- Use dialogue to help bring characters or situations to life.
- Use a variety of sentence lengths to make the description more interesting to read, e.g. short sentences to add tension / complex sentences to build description.

Descriptive Writing

Describing Scenes

Read these two descriptions of the same scene. Which do you think gives the most vivid impression of the scene and why?

You might have found the second version more effective because it gives a more vivid impression of the state of the room.

💡 *Can you see what techniques the writer has used to create this effect?*

Here are some ideas:
- Adverbs have been used, e.g. to describe how Jane's parents looked – looked *angrily*.
- Adjectives have been used to add to the description, e.g. *terrible* mess, *unidentified* liquid, *beige* carpet.
- Similes have been used, e.g. 'it looked as if someone had emptied several dustbins over it'.
- Dialogue has been used to create a sense of Jane's father's reaction to the scene.
- Use of the senses.
- Long, complex sentences to build description.

When Jane's parents returned home they looked at the state that they found in the living room. They were shocked by the mess it had been left in after the party. The floor was littered with rubbish and there were cans everywhere. Some kind of liquid had been spilt on the carpet and had left a large stain on it and the dining table had a scratch across it. The air was stale and stuffy. Jane's dad shouted for her to come down straight away.

When Jane's parent's returned home early they looked angrily at what they found in the living room. They were visibly shocked by the terrible mess it had been left in after the party the previous evening. The floor was so littered with rubbish it looked as if someone had emptied several dustbins over it and there were coke and lemonade cans everywhere. Some kind of unidentified liquid had been spilt on the beige carpet and had left a large, purple stain on it, which had spread like a big blot on blotting paper. The dining table had a deep scratch right across the middle of it. The air was stale and stuffy and smelt like a rugby team's changing room after a particularly hard match.' I don't believe this!' exclaimed Jane's dad, in disbelief.' Jane! Get down here. Now!'

Setting and Mood

Language can be used in different ways to create a sense of setting and mood. Look at the following description and think about the kind of **setting** and **mood** the writer creates and the ways he uses language to create his effects.

> *Coming up for Air* by George Orwell
>
> Thursday was market day. Chaps with round red faces like pumpkins and dirty smocks and huge boots covered with dry cow-dung, carrying long hazel switches, used to drive their brutes into the market-place early in the morning. For hours there'd be a terrific hullabaloo: dogs barking, pigs squealing, chaps in tradesmen's vans who wanted to get through the crush cracking their whips and cursing, and everyone who had anything to do with the cattle shouting and throwing sticks.

You might have noted some of these ideas:
- The setting described is that of a busy cattle market and the writer creates a mood of the bustle and action taking place there.
- As well as describing the visual scene, the writer uses sound and onomatopoeia, e.g. 'barking', 'squealing', 'cracking'.
- Adjectives are used, e.g. *red* faces, *huge* boots.
- A simile is used: 'faces like pumpkins'.

Characters and Actions

The following writer adopts a different style to create a picture of his subject.

 How do you think this differs from the previous extract by George Orwell?

> *Return of the Native* by Thomas Hardy
>
> Along the road walked an old man. He was white-headed as a mountain, bowed in the shoulders, and faded in general aspect. He wore a glazed hat, an ancient boat-cloak, and shoes; his brass buttons bearing an anchor upon their face. In his hand was a silver-headed walking stick, which he used as a veritable third leg, perseveringly dotting the ground with its point at every few inches' interval. One would have said that he had been, in his day, a naval officer of some sort or other.

You might have noticed here that the writer focuses simply on the visual detail of what the character looked like and what he was doing.

Some adjectives are used to give more detail, e.g. *old* man, *ancient* boat-cloak, and a simile is also used to make this visual description more vivid: 'white-headed as a mountain'.

Quick Test

Complete the sentences below.
1. Adverbs might be used in descriptive writing to tell you more about the _____.
2. You use onomatopoeia in writing to create a sense of _____.
3. Description can be used to create an impression of setting and _____.

KEY WORDS
Make sure you understand these words before moving on!
- Characters
- Description
- Convincing
- Observation
- Language
- Thesaurus
- Techniques
- Adverbs
- Adjectives
- Similes
- Metaphors
- Onomatopoeia
- Vocabulary
- Dictionary
- Dialogue
- Setting
- Mood

Descriptive Writing

Key Words Exercise

Work out the key words from the clues below, then find them in the word search.

1. Another word for speech.

2. Description can help create a sense of _____ and _____.

3. Description can help you create convincing _____.

4. Good description is often based on careful _____.

5. Effective description can make your characters more _____.

6. Vivid _____ can create a strong impression of setting and mood.

7. To write descriptively you need to choose your _____ carefully.

8. A _____ and a _____ can help you choose the right words to use.

9. Your writing is more effective if you use a variety of _____.

10. These words describe verbs.

11. Both _____ and _____ use comparisons to make writing more vivid.

12. These words describe nouns.

13. _____ is used to create a sense of sound.

14. Another word for the words you use is _____.

C	H	A	R	A	C	T	E	R	S	N	A	T	Y	S
V	O	N	O	M	A	T	O	P	O	E	I	A	R	W
Q	L	M	E	T	A	P	H	O	R	S	M	F	A	I
P	D	S	Y	O	W	G	J	U	T	J	H	O	N	A
O	E	T	E	C	H	N	I	Q	U	E	S	X	O	U
O	S	A	T	S	E	T	T	I	N	G	E	T	I	D
B	C	V	O	T	B	U	L	A	T	C	V	H	T	G
S	R	Q	L	A	T	N	U	I	S	O	O	E	C	A
E	I	V	B	N	G	I	B	Y	O	N	C	S	I	D
R	P	S	O	M	T	M	N	I	R	V	A	A	D	J
V	T	B	M	A	Z	A	T	G	E	I	B	U	C	E
A	I	K	S	I	M	I	L	E	S	N	U	R	Y	C
T	O	C	M	L	E	R	S	T	U	C	L	U	C	T
I	N	N	L	I	Y	M	I	L	E	I	A	S	Y	I
O	L	A	D	V	E	R	B	S	S	N	R	W	R	V
N	D	I	A	L	O	G	U	E	I	G	Y	H	L	E
I	O	H	I	T	U	L	A	N	G	U	A	G	E	S

Testing Understanding

1 Look at the following passage from *The Trumpet Major* by Thomas Hardy, which describes a character, Anne. Make a list of the techniques that Hardy uses to make his description of Anne vivid and effective. Give an example from the passage of each technique you have listed.

Anne was fair, very fair, in a poetic sense; but in complexion she was of that particular tint between blonde and brunette which is inconveniently left without a name. Her eyes were honest and inquiring, her mouth cleanly cut and yet not classical, the middle point of her upper lip scarcely descending so far as it should have done by rights, so that at the merest pleasant thought, not to mention a smile, portions of two or three white teeth were uncovered whether she would or not. Some people said that this was very attractive. She was graceful and slender, and, though but little above five feet in height, could draw herself up to look tall. In her manner, in her comings and goings, in her 'I'll do this,' or 'I'll do that,' she combined dignity with sweetness as no other girl could do; and any impressionable stranger youths who passed by were led to yearn for a windfall of speech from her, and to see at the same time that they would not get it. In short, beneath all that was charming and simple in this young woman there lurked a real firmness, unperceived at first, as the speck of colour lurks unperceived in the heart of the palest parsley flower.

She wore a white handkerchief to cover her white neck, and a cap on her head with a pink ribbon round it, tied in a bow at the front. She had a great variety of these cap-ribbons, the young men being fond of sending them to her as presents until they fell definitely in love with a special sweetheart elsewhere, when they left off doing so. Between the border of her cap and her forehead were ranged a row of round brown curls, like swallows' nests under eaves.

2 Now look at this passage (also from *The Trumpet Major*) in which Hardy describes the setting. Make a list of the techniques he uses to create an impression of the setting and a sense of the atmosphere.

Immediately before her was the large, smooth mill-pond, over-full, and intruding into the hedge and into the road. The water, with its flowing leaves and spots of froth, was stealing away, like Time, under the dark arch, to tumble over the great slimy wheel within. On the other side of the mill-pond was an open place called the Cross, because it was three-quarters of one, two lanes and a cattle-drive meeting there. It was the general rendezvous and arena of the surrounding village. Behind this a steep slope rose high into the sky, merging in a wide and open down, now littered with sheep newly shorn. The upland by its height completely sheltered the mill and village from north winds, making summers of springs, reducing winters to autumn temperatures, and permitting myrtle to flourish in the open air.

The heaviness of noon pervaded the scene, and under its influence the sheep had ceased to feed. Nobody was standing at the Cross, the few inhabitants being indoors at their dinner. No human being was on the down, and no human eye or interest but Anne's seemed to be concerned with it. The bees still worked on, and the butterflies did not rest from roving, their smallness seeming to shield them from the stagnating effect that this turning moment of day had on larger creatures. Otherwise all was still.

Descriptive Writing

Write a piece of descriptive writing of your own on each of the following ideas:

- **A person you have met.**
- **A view or place you have seen.**
- **An experience you have had.**

Try to make each of your pieces of writing as vivid as possible by using some of the following techniques:

- Imagery such as similes and metaphors to help your readers re-create your description in their own minds.
- The use of the senses to create a vivid impression of the sights, sounds, tastes, smells and feelings.
- The use of adverbs and adjectives.
- The use of dialogue.
- A range of sentence lengths.

When you have written your pieces, read each one aloud to a partner and discuss with your partner how effectively your description came across.

Ask your partner to comment on the following:

- Your use of language.
- The techniques you have used to describe your subject.
- Ways that you could improve your description.

When you have done that, switch roles and listen to your partner's descriptions and comment in the same way on their piece of writing.

What is Covered in this Topic?

This topic looks at...
- different kinds of sentences
- simple sentences
- the verb in a sentence
- verb and subject agreement.

Different Kinds of Sentences

There are four different kinds of sentences. Each type of sentence has a particular purpose.

Most of the sentences that you use in your writing are statement sentences.

Note that sentences that are exclamations end with an exclamation mark.

Some commands can also end with exclamation marks.

Type of Sentence	Purpose	Examples
Statement	To make a statement	• I love reading novels. • It is sunny today.
Command (sometimes called imperatives)	To command, order or request	• Come down here now. • Pass me the milk please. • Go over there.
Question	To ask a question	• Did you enjoy the film? • Have you finished your work yet?
Exclamation	To express surprise, anger, pleasure, etc.	• What a lovely day it is! • How clever you are!

Cinema

Did you enjoy the film?

Sentences 1

Simple Sentences

The most basic kind of sentence is the **simple** sentence.

Simple sentences have...
- a **subject**
- a **verb** (a verb that has a subject is called a **finite** verb).

Lots of problems that can occur when writing sentences are to do with these parts of the sentence. It's important that you're able to identify the subject and the verb in your sentences so that you can check that you're using correct grammar and English in your writing.

Identifying the Subject

The subject tells you who or what the sentence is about. The position of the subject in a sentence can vary.

Usually the subject comes at the beginning of a sentence:

Subject   Verb

Tom trains hard on his mountain bike.

Sometimes the subject comes a little later:

Subject   Verb

On the whole Samira likes science.

Occasionally the subject comes after the verb:

Verb   Subject

In the middle of the pitch lay an injured player.

The subject can be a single word, e.g. 'Tom' or 'Samira' or a group of words, e.g. 'an injured player' – this group of words is called a **phrase**.

Identifying the Verb

In a statement sentence the verb normally comes immediately after the subject:

Subject Verb

David thinks that computer games are really fun.

Sometimes, though, there are one or more words between the subject and the verb:

Subject   Verb

Nick, surprisingly, did better in the test than Susie.

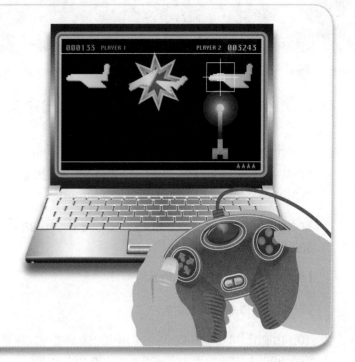

What Verbs Tell You

The verb tells you about the subject and can give different kinds of information:
- It can describe an **action**, e.g. 'trains', 'works'.
- It can describe a **state** or **condition**, e.g. 'likes', 'hates'.
- Some verbs simply link the subject to the rest of the sentence, for example:

Subject Verb Rest of sentence

Helen is **on holiday in Cornwall.**

Here is another example:

Subject Verb Rest of sentence

Kate was **very happy with the money.**

Other linking verbs that work like this include 'seems', 'appears', 'becomes', 'am', 'are'.

The verb in a sentence can consist of one word, e.g. thinks, or a group of words (called a verb phrase), for example:

Subject   Verb phrase

George **shouldn't have been going** **on the trip.**

Sentences 1

Subject and Verb Agreement

When writing a sentence the subject and verb must **agree**. Mistakes often happen in written sentences because there isn't agreement.

Look at these two sentences and see if you can see what is wrong with them.

I were walking to the shops.

My books is on the table.

You might have noticed that in these two sentences, the subject and verb do not agree.

I were (✗) walking to the shops should be:

I was (✓) walking to the shops.

My books is (✗) on the table should be:

My books are (✓) on the table.

In spoken English, it's quite common for verbs and subjects not to be in agreement, but in written English it's not considered correct.

Quick Test

1. How many kinds of sentences are there?
2. What is another name for a command?
3. A group of words is called a

   _____ .

4. A verb that has a subject is called a

   _____ verb.

Key Words Exercise

Complete each sentence by finding the missing word.

1. The most basic kind of sentence is called a _____ sentence.

2. A group of words without a verb is not a _____ .

3. For a sentence to be written in correct English the verb and subject must _____ .

4. A verb that has a subject is called a _____ verb.

5. 'Are you ready yet?' is an example of a _____ .

6. When a verb tells you what someone is doing it describes an _____ .

7. If the verb in a sentence is made up of more than one word it is called a verb _____ .

8. Apart from describing actions a verb can also describe a _____ or _____ .

9. 'Oh no, I've torn my coat!' is an example of an _____ .

10. Every sentence must have a _____ and a _____ .

11. A sentence that issues an order is called a _____ or an _____ .

12. 'I like school.' is an example of a _____ sentence.

Sentences 1

1 **Identify the types of sentences:**

a) Clean up your room immediately!

b) I think autumn is my favourite time of the year.

c) Could you lend me five pounds to go out tonight, please?

d) Pass me that pan, would you?

e) The sun was shining brightly and I felt happy and free.

f) That plate was very hot!

g) Please make sure that you wipe your feet on the mat.

h) What a silly boy you are!

2 **Identify the subject and verb in these sentences:**

a) Joe ran as quickly as he could to the bus stop.

b) It was hard but Rachael passed her exam.

c) In the corner of the room sat an evil old witch.

d) Harry and Mario camped by the river.

e) In the middle of the table stood a large, silver candlestick.

f) Annie is happy with her watch.

g) Sam threw the ball into the middle of the crowd.

h) Gasping for breath Kim crossed the finish line.

i) The boat sank in the stormy sea.

j) Sandra and Steph are from Durham.

3 **Identify which of these sentences are incorrect and write out the corrected sentence.**

a) We are going on a long walk tomorrow.

b) You is a good student and work very hard.

c) I am a keen cyclist.

d) I thought you was going to help me tidy up.

e) I were going to go out tonight but I haven't any money.

f) My dogs has two meals a day.

g) There is lots of people queuing for tickets.

h) We was going to the seaside.

Skills Practice

Work with a partner to design a poster to show the four different kinds of sentences.

Your poster should...
- be eye-catching
- be clear and easy to understand
- give an example of each kind of sentence
- use layout effectively to display information.

Now create a second poster that shows how simple sentences are structured and how to identify the subject and verb.

Your poster should...
- give clear information
- show examples
- present the information in an interesting way.

Extension Activity

Present your posters to your class and ask them to comment on how effectively they think that you have presented the information.

Ask them to give examples of the ways you might improve the posters (if there are any).

Sentences 2

This topic looks at...
- compound sentences
- phrases and clauses
- complex sentences.

Compound Sentences

When two or more simple sentences are joined together by connectives (also called conjunctions), compound sentences are formed.

The conjunctions that join simple sentences together are called coordinating conjunctions or coordinators.

simple sentence

Jasmine worked hard on her essay.

She got full marks for it.

simple sentence

compound sentence

Jasmine worked hard on her essay and she got full marks for it.

coordinating conjunction

Here are some more examples of simple sentences made into compound sentences by connecting them with conjunctions:
- I want to go to the party *but* I haven't finished my homework.
- Amy found delivering papers hard work *yet* she enjoyed it.
- We got a bus to town *then* went to the cinema.

Types of Conjunctions

Conjunctions that join simple sentences together are: 'but', 'or', 'nor', 'then', 'yet', 'for', 'so', 'and'.

Sometimes you can slightly change the meaning of the sentence depending on which coordinating conjunction you use. For example...

- I am going to visit Todd. I will see Michaela.
  - I am going to visit Todd *and* I will see Michaela.
  - I am going to visit Todd *then* I will see Michaela.
  - I am going to visit Todd *so* I will see Michaela.

💡 *Think about the differences in meaning of these sentences depending on which coordinating conjunctions have been used.*

Phrases and Clauses

A **phrase** is a group of words that doesn't contain a finite verb and so doesn't make complete sense on its own.

For example...
- at great cost
- cycling furiously
- to my great relief
- with a silly grin.

A **clause** is a group of words that contains a finite verb. A simple sentence contains one clause.

Multiple Sentences

Sentences that contain more than one clause are called **multiple sentences**.

Compound sentences contain two clauses, so are multiple sentences. Every clause must contain a finite verb.

Look at this example of a multiple sentence:

Mallory rushed to the window but he saw nothing

finite verb   finite verb

To check whether a sentence is a simple sentence or a multiple sentence, you need to pick out the finite verbs. If there is only one, it's a simple sentence. If there is more than one, it's a multiple sentence.

Sentences 2

Main and Subordinate Clauses

Some clauses can make complete sense on their own. These are called **main clauses**. Other clauses can't stand on their own because they are **incomplete**. These are called **subordinate clauses**.

subordinate clause	main clause

Although he tried hard | **Mark failed his driving test.**

The main clause is '*Mark failed his driving test*' as it makes complete sense on its own.

The subordinate clause is '*Although he tried hard*' as it's incomplete and can't make sense on its own.

Differences Between Sentences

Look at these two simple sentences:

The band played well. They lost the competition.

The same information in a compound sentence could read:

The band played well but they lost the competition.

A **complex sentence** has one main clause and one or more subordinate clauses. Complex sentences join the different parts of a sentence in a way that gives you more information than if you wrote in simple sentences.

BATTLE
of the Bands

Friday, 29th May, 9pm

Writing Complex Sentences

A complex sentence can present information in several ways, each of which gives a slightly different meaning.

💡 *Think about the different meanings of these complex sentences.*

main clause	subordinate clause

(The band played well) (even though they lost the competition.)

subordinate clause	main clause

(Even though the band played well) (they lost the competition.)

subordinate clause	main clause

(Although the band played well) (they lost the competition.)

Each sentence has one main clause that can stand on its own and one subordinate clause that can't because it's incomplete.

Interesting and varied writing makes use of a variety of sentence types, and in order to write accurately and express your ideas well you need to use sentences correctly.

Quick Test

1. What is a phrase?
2. When writing why should you use a variety of sentence types?
3. What joins two simple sentences together to make a compound sentence?
4. How many main clauses does a complex sentence have?

KEY WORDS

Make sure you understand these words before moving on!

- Simple sentence
- Compound sentence
- Coordinating conjunction
- Phrase
- Clause
- Multiple sentence
- Main clause
- Incomplete
- Subordinate clause
- Complex sentence

Sentences 2

Match each key word with its definition.

| Complex sentence | A sentence with one main clause and any number of subordinate clauses. |

| Main clause | A group of words that doesn't contain a finite verb. |

| Phrase | A sentence made up of two simple sentences. |

| Simple sentence | Joins two sentences together. |

| Coordinating conjunction | A sentence with just one finite verb. |

| Compound sentence | A group of words with a finite verb. |

| Multiple sentence | A clause that doesn't make complete sense on its own. |

| Subordinate clause | A sentence that contains more than one finite verb. |

| Clause | A clause that has a finite verb and subject and makes complete sense on its own. |

1 **Use suitable coordinating conjunctions to change these simple sentences into compound sentences.**

a) I didn't know about the problem. I can't explain it.

b) She ran for the bus. She missed it.

c) Shall we go to the cinema? Shall we go bowling?

d) We must leave now. We will miss the start.

e) I will tidy up my bedroom. I don't want to.

f) I will see you tonight. I will pick you up at 7.00pm.

2 **What is the difference in meaning between these pairs of sentences?**

a) Sam didn't revise much for his exam and he got a grade C.
Sam didn't revise much for his exam but he got a grade C.

b) We went to drama club and had some hot dogs and pop.
We went to drama club then had some hot dogs and pop.

3 **Which of these are phrases and which are clauses?**

a) swerving round the bend

b) I love going on trips

c) you did well

d) coming out

e) you drive me mad

4 **Identify the main clause and subordinate clause in the following sentences.**

a) I put on my coat because it was raining.

b) As the door was locked he couldn't get in.

c) Before opening his notebook he sharpened his pencil.

d) He was slumped in the chair staring vacantly at the television.

e) I paid the bill although the food was disgusting.

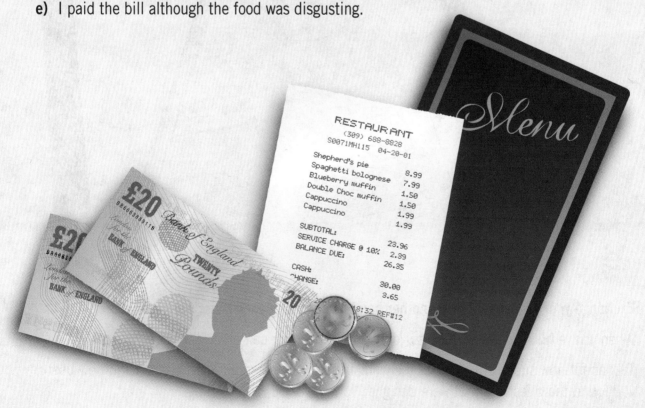

Sentences 2

Work with a partner to devise a set of worksheets explaining compound sentences and complex sentences.

Your worksheets should…
* explain things accurately
* be clear and easy to understand
* give an example of each kind of sentence
* use layout effectively to display information
* contain at least three questions to test understanding.

Write an answer sheet to go with your test questions.

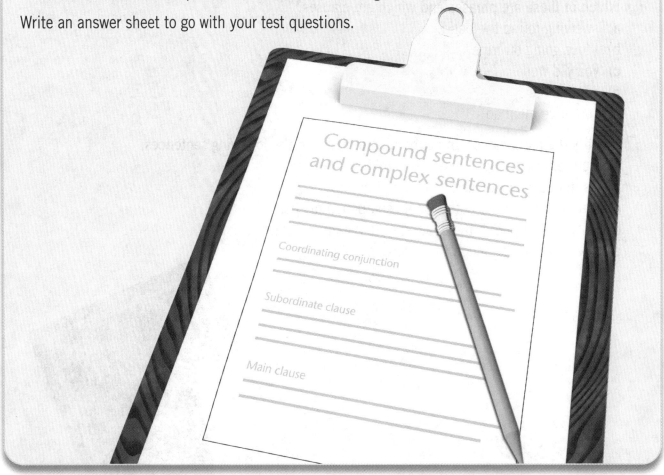

Exchange your worksheets with another pair and try doing each other's worksheets.

When you've finished the worksheets, join up with the other pair and discuss how you got on.

Talk about how successful you felt the worksheets were in explaining the ideas and how useful you found the questions that were designed to test your understanding.

Writing Formal Letters

What is Covered in this Topic?

This topic looks at...
- the purposes of writing formal letters
- setting out a letter
- using language.

Formal Letters

Although communication by e-mail is very common nowadays, letters of all kinds are still written and received everyday. Some are handwritten (in fact some job advertisements still ask for a handwritten letter of application), but the vast majority are word processed and some letters are mass produced.

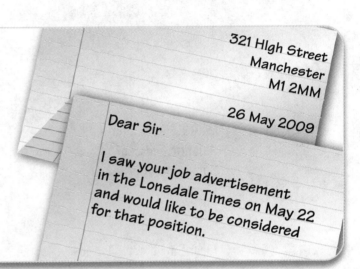

> 321 High Street
> Manchester
> M1 2MM
>
> 26 May 2009
>
> Dear Sir
>
> I saw your job advertisement in the Lonsdale Times on May 22 and would like to be considered for that position.

The Purposes of Formal Letters

Formal (or 'business') letters are written for a wide variety of purposes.

Here are some of the purposes:

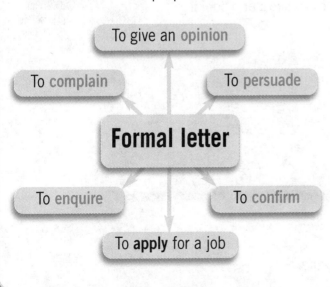

To give an opinion

To complain — To persuade

Formal letter

To enquire — To confirm

To **apply** for a job

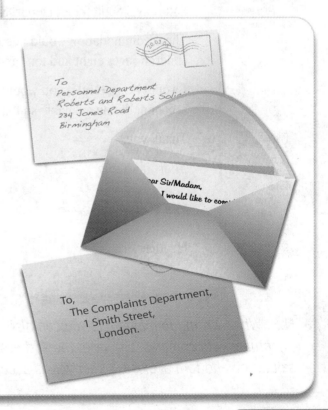

> To
> Personnel Department
> Roberts and Roberts Solici...
> 234 Jones Road
> Birmingham

> ...ar Sir/Madam,
> ...I would like to com...

> To,
> The Complaints Department,
> 1 Smith Street,
> London.

Writing Formal Letters

How to Lay Out a Formal Letter

Here is an example of a formal letter.

💡 *What elements do you notice?*

2 Barton Road
Slingsby
Brampton
Lancs
BS 2 ISR

Writer's address

7 May 2009

Date

West Land Holidays
Atlantic Crescent
Sunnington-on-Sea
Cumbria
CB5 7UR

Address of the person you're writing to – sometimes called the 'recipient'

Dear Sir

Addresses the person you're writing to – sometimes called the 'salutation'

I am writing to enquire if you have a holiday flat available for early September, this year. The dates I require are as follows: Arrive on Saturday 3 September; Depart Saturday 10 September.

The accommodation would need to sleep four adults and two children (ages eight and ten) and we would need three bedrooms.

The content is to the point and clearly expresses dates and requirements

I would be grateful if you would let me know if you have suitable accommodation available so that I can make a firm booking.

Thank you.

Polite

Yours faithfully

Formal close – 'Yours faithfully' matches 'Dear Sir' opening

Heather Brown

Heather Brown

Signature

N.B. When writing formal letters you can also punctuate with commas, e.g. after the address, salutation and formal close. Either way is acceptable.

Features of a Formal Letter

Note the following features:
- Your address goes at the top on the right hand side.
- The address is followed by the date.
- The address you're writing to goes on the left hand side (it can either be positioned directly opposite your address or positioned opposite and below, as shown on page 26. It should be one or the other, though, not half and half.)
- The letter begins 'Dear Sir'. If you don't know the name of the person you're writing to then you should use either 'Dear Sir' or 'Dear Madam'. This formal opening is sometimes called the 'salutation'.
- The content of the letter is clear and all the necessary information is given in a concise way.
- The 'Thank you' is not essential but it adds an extra element of politeness to the tone.
- The formal close of 'Yours faithfully' matches the opening.

Faithfully or Sincerely?

If you don't use the person's name, e.g. 'Dear Sir / Madam', you should always end your letter 'Yours faithfully'.

If you use the person's name, e.g. 'Dear Mr / Mrs / Miss / Ms _____', you should always end your letter 'Yours sincerely'.

Getting the Tone Right

When writing a letter it's very important that you choose your language carefully to get the tone right.

Whatever your purpose in writing the letter, you're likely to get a much better response if you use a polite tone.

Even if you're complaining you still need to be polite. If you're unpleasant or abusive, the person reading your letter isn't likely to want to help you.

Spelling and Punctuation

How you write your letter says something about you. As well as getting the tone right it's important that you check that your spelling and punctuation are correct.

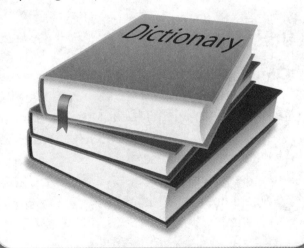

Writing Formal Letters

Letters of Complaint

Look at the following example:

Heather Brown succeeded in booking her holiday, but unfortunately things didn't go as smoothly as she had hoped and so she had to write to complain to the company.

Here are two possible approaches she might have taken. Which do you think is the most effective?

Mr. D. James
James Travel Agents
11 High Street
LONDON

Dear Mr James

I am writing to complain about the holiday flat booked through your company that we used for our family holiday two weeks ago. I can honestly say that I have never stayed in such a dump in all my life. It was like a slum and hardly anything worked. Your brochure said it was well equipped but that was rubbish because it wasn't.

I would like you to give me my money back or I will never book with you again.

Yours sincerely

Heather Brown

Dear Mr James

I would like to complain about the holiday flat that we stayed in recently and booked through your company. Unfortunately the flat did not live up to the description in your brochure. It was clear that the flat had not been properly cleaned as the carpet and some of the crockery was dirty. The light in one of the bedrooms did not work and the grill on the oven was broken. There were only three glasses and two teaspoons even though the flat was meant to sleep six people.

I'm sure that you will agree that this is not satisfactory and would be grateful if you would look into the matter for me. Under the circumstances I feel that a refund of at least part of the rental fee would be justified.

Yours sincerely

Heather Brown

Quick Test

1. What goes under your address on a letter?
2. If you began a letter 'Dear Mrs Nugent' how would you end it?
3. When would you use 'Yours faithfully'?
4. Where does your address go on a letter?

KEY WORDS

Make sure you understand these words before moving on!

- Application
- Formal
- Business
- Complain
- Opinion
- Persuade
- Confirm
- Enquire
- Address
- Date
- Salutation
- Content
- Faithfully
- Sincerely
- Language
- Tone
- Polite

Unscramble these anagrams and link them to the correct definition.

When applying for a job your letter of application should be a _____ letter.

If you use the person's name you should end your letter 'Yours _____.'

NICELYRES

Another term for a formal letter is a _____ letter.

ATED

You should put the _____ under the address.

SADREDS

If you're not happy with something you might write a letter to _____.

PIELOT

ENTO

In the top right hand side you put your _____.

AHFITLYFLU

When you apply for a job you usually write a letter of _____.

NOTCENT

In a letter you should always be _____.

ASNAILTOUT

MONCRIF

If you want someone to agree with your view you try to _____ them.

QUIREEN

Choosing the right words is important to get the right _____.

ADRUPEES

INPOINO

In a letter you might express your own _____.

CAPTAINPOIL

If you begin a letter 'Dear Sir' or 'Dear Madam' you should end it 'Yours _____.'

MANICLOP

If you want to find something out you might _____ about it.

SUBSINES

RALFOM

What you write in your letter is called the _____.

If you want to make sure you're booked on a holiday you would write to _____ the dates and other details.

The formal opening part of the letter is known as the _____.

Writing Formal Letters

Read the following letter carefully and identify any mistakes or problems that you find in it.

> 7 Dymock Road
> Haweschester
> Buckdenshire
> HW4 2RT
>
> Zippo Computers
> 18 Cockerbury Trading Park
> Wetherbury
> Northshire
> WE3 6TU
>
> Dear Sir
>
> I recently bought a new series 1000 XPZ laptop computer from you by mail order. Unfortunatly something seems to have gone wrong with it. When I switch it on their is a loud buzzing sound, the screen goes blue and then the computer shuts down. I rung youre customer services depatment and thay said I needed to write to you explaining the problem.
>
> I think this is rubbish service and you had better do something about it.
>
> Yours sincerely
>
> *I. M. Moody*
>
> I. M. Moody

Skills Practice

1 **Write a letter complaining about something that you have bought recently that has proved to be faulty.**

In your letter make sure that you…
- explain the problem clearly and straightforwardly
- state when and where you bought the item
- say what you would expect them to do
- use a polite and reasonable tone throughout.

2 **Write a letter to a travel company confirming your holiday booking.**

You should make sure that you cover the following points in your letter:
- The exact dates of your holiday – making sure that your arrival and departure dates are clearly stated.
- The accommodation that you have booked, e.g. the number of bedrooms, facilities, etc.
- The number of adults and children that will be arriving.
- Any other information that you think is important.

Extension Activity

Create a poster for your classroom wall showing how to write a formal letter.

Your poster should give an example of a formal letter (choose your own topic for the letter) and all features should be clearly labelled.

The features should cover the following:
- Correct positioning and layout of addresses
- Date
- Salutation
- Content to suit purpose and audience
- The formal ending (giving alternatives according to salutation).

Your poster should also include between four and six bullet points giving the key points to remember when writing a formal letter.

Novels and Short Stories

What is Covered in this Topic?

This topic looks at...
- the features of novels and short stories
- approaches to studying your text
- analysing characters.

Features of Novels and Short Stories

Novels and short stories have many things in common – the main difference is, as you might guess, that short stories are a lot shorter than novels. Other than that, though, both...
- tell stories created out of the writer's imagination
- want to interest and entertain the reader
- usually contain characters
- usually use dialogue
- often explore various ideas or themes.

Approaching your Text

When you're studying a novel or a short story, (often called a text) the first thing you need to do is to read it so that you get a clear idea of what it's about and the storyline or plot.

Here are some things that you can do while you're reading your text, which will help later when you come to study it in more detail:

- Keep a 'log' of your ideas on the text as you read it – jotting a few brief points in a notebook.
- Jot down your ideas or anything interesting that you've noticed about the characters.
- Note down anything that strikes you about the setting or atmosphere.
- Note down anything that catches your attention about the language that's used – maybe a particular piece of description or a phrase or image that you found striking.

Understanding your Text

Here's one approach you could use to help you develop your understanding of the text.

Read through the novel or short story to get an overall picture of the story.

Look at how the writer opens the story.

As you're reading it, make a brief summary of each chapter – just pick out the key points.

To get an overview you need to have a clear idea of the plot, characters and ideas that the writer explores.

Think about the narrative viewpoint (or perspective) – is the story told in the first person (I) or the third person (he, she)?

Have ideas about the characters – who they are, how they act, what they do, how they relate to other characters and look at the way the writer describes them.

Look at how the writer creates an impression of the setting of the story – look at the language used to describe it.

Look at how the writer ends the story.

Novels and Short Stories

Analysing Characters

Characters in novels and short stories aren't real people, but the writer wants to create an impression of them that makes them believable and convincing to you.

When you're asked to **analyse** characters in a story you're really being asked to look at the ways writers use language to give you an impression of them.

In order to do this, you need to understand some of the methods and **techniques** that writers can use to create characters and present them to you through the story.

How Writers Create Characters

Look at the following two passages in which Charles Dickens presents different characters.

 What impression do you form of each character? What techniques does the writer use?

Hard Times by Charles Dickens

He was a rich man: banker, merchant, manufacturer, and what not. A big, loud man, with a stare and a metallic laugh. A man made out of a coarse material, which seemed to have been stretched to make so much of him. A man with a great puffed head and forehead, swelled veins in his temples, and such a strained skin to his face that it seemed to hold his eyes open and lift his eyebrows up. A man with a pervading appearance on him of being inflated like a balloon, and ready to start. A man who could never sufficiently vaunt himself a self-made man. A man who was always proclaiming, through that brassy speaking-trumpet of a voice of his, his old ignorance and his old poverty. A man who was the Bull of humility.

A year or two younger than his eminently practical friend, Mr Bounderby looked older; his seven or eight and forty might have had the seven or eight added to it again, without surprising anybody. He had not much hair. One might have fancied he had talked it off; and that what was left, all standing up in disorder, was in that condition from being constantly blown about by his windy boastfulness.

Great Expectations by Charles Dickens

She was dressed in rich materials – satins, and lace, and silks – all of white. Her shoes were white. And she had a long white veil dependent from her hair, and she had bridal flowers in her hair, but her hair was white. Some bright jewels sparkled on her neck and on her hands, and some other jewels lay sparkling on the table.

Dresses, less splendid than the dress she wore, and half-packed trunks, were scattered about. She had not quite finished dressing, for she had but one shoe on – the other was on the table near her hand – her veil was but half arranged, her watch and chain were not put on, and some lace for her bosom lay with those trinkets, and with her handkerchief, and gloves, and some flowers, and a Prayer-book, all confusedly heaped about the looking-glass.

It was not in the first few moments that I saw all these things, though I saw more of them in the first moments than might be supposed. But, I saw that everything within my view which ought to be white, had been white long ago, and had lost its lustre, and was faded and yellow. I saw that the bride within the bridal dress had withered like the dress, and like the flowers, and had no brightness left but the brightness of her sunken eyes. I saw that the dress had been put upon the rounded figure of a young woman, and that the figure upon which it now hung loose, had shrunk to skin and bone.

Here are some ideas you might have noted about *Hard Times*:

- Details are given about Bounderby's status and profession.
- His physical appearance and size are stressed, e.g. 'big', 'a stare', 'great puffed head', 'swelled veins' and a simile is used to emphasise this further with the description of him 'being inflated like a balloon'.
- The sounds he makes are also emphasised, e.g. 'metallic laugh', a 'loud man', 'brassy speaking-trumpet voice'.
- We get the impression of a loud, brash, boastful and bullying kind of man.

Here are some ideas you might have noted about *Great Expectations*:

- Dickens contrasts the narrator's initial impression with what he sees as he looks more closely at the woman.
- At first he sees rich satins, laces and silks and bright jewels on the woman's neck and hands.
- He then sees that everything that should be white has become yellowed with age, the flowers withered and the woman old and shrunken.
- The woman is described through her clothing and jewellery. The vividness is achieved through the use of a variety of adjectives, e.g. 'rich materials', 'bright jewels', 'sunken eyes'.

In summary, writers use the following techniques:

- Description – often writers describe what their characters look like, how they dress, how they walk, etc.
- Actions – you also learn about characters through what they do, how they act and how they behave in the story.
- Dialogue – what the characters say and how they say it can add to your impression of a character.
- Feelings – the writer can tell us what a character feels or thinks.

Quick Test

1. Novels and short stories should capture the reader's _____.
2. What is one of the main purposes of novels and short stories?
3. The ideas that novels explore are called _____.
4. Another word that means the same as storyline is _____.

Novels and Short Stories

Key Words Exercise

Work out the key words from the clues below, then copy and complete the crossword.

ACROSS

2. Narrative _____. (9)

4. Books that you read are these. (5)

6. Ideas in a story. (6)

7. Spoken words. (8)

10. A long story. (5)

11. A story but not a novel. (5)

14. Good stories _____ the reader. (8)

15. The purpose of a novel is to _____. (9)

16. 'I like this work.' is written in the first _____. (6)

DOWN

1. You could 'cut it with a knife'. (10)

3. Writers use this when writing stories. (11)

5. It wasn't first, it wasn't second but it was _____ person. (5)

6. Writers use a variety of these. (10)

8. Storyline. (4)

9. These need to be convincing. (10)

12. When you look at a story closely you _____ it. (7)

13. Where it all happens. (7)

Testing Understanding

Look at the following extract from *Of Mice and Men* by John Steinbeck in which he describes two characters. Read the extract carefully and answer the questions that follow.

1. What aspect of the characters does Steinbeck focus on to begin with?

2. What is your impression of the first man and how is language used to create this impression? Gives specific examples of language used and the effects created.

3. How does the second man contrast with the first? What is your impression of him and how is language used to create this impression?

4. Which of these characters do you think is the dominant one and why?

5. What does the dialogue tell you about the characters?

For a moment the place was lifeless, and then two men emerged from the path and came into the opening by the green pool. They had walked in single file down the path, and even in the open one stayed behind the other. Both were dressed in denim trousers and in denim coats with brass buttons. Both wore black, shapeless hats and both carried tight blanket rolls slung over their shoulders. The first man was small and quick, dark of face, with restless eyes and sharp, strong features. Every part of him was defined: small, strong hands, slender arms, a thin and bony nose. Behind him walked his opposite, a huge man, shapeless of face, with large, pale eyes, with wide, sloping shoulders; and he walked heavily, dragging his feet a little, the way a bear drags his paws. His arms did not swing at his sides, but hung loosely and only moved because the heavy hands were pendula.

The first man stopped short in the clearing, and the follower nearly ran over him. He took off his hat and wiped the sweat-band with his forefinger and snapped the moisture off. His huge companion dropped his blankets and flung himself down and drank from the surface of the green pool; drank with long gulps, snorting into the water like a horse. The small man stepped nervously beside him.

'Lennie!' he said sharply. 'Lennie, for God's sakes don't drink so much.' Lennie continued to snort into the pool. The small man leaned over and shook him by the shoulder. 'Lennie. You gonna be sick like you was last night.'

Lennie dipped his whole head under, hat and all, and then he sat up on the bank and his hat dripped down on his blue coat and ran down his back. 'Tha's good,' he said. 'You drink some, George. You take a good big drink.' He smiled happily.

Novels and Short Stories

Pick a novel or short story that you have read, either as part of your English lessons or as part of your own private reading. (You can choose more than one story if you want to.)

Pick out three characters from your chosen novel or short story.

For each character select a passage from the novel or story where the writer describes your selected character.

Write an analysis of each passage showing how the writer presents the character.

You should write about the following:
- The impression you form of the character.
- The techniques the writer uses to create a sense of character.
- How language is used to create effects.

Remember to give examples of language used and the effects created to support the points you make.

Extension Activity

Pick one of your characters and draw a picture of him or her based on the description given in the novel or story. You might find it useful to use a large sheet of paper for your drawing – it doesn't have to be a brilliant artistic work – you could even use a 'cartoon' approach.

Around your picture of the character you could put quotations that you have picked out from the text that describe the character and have helped you to visualise him or her.

Presenting Information

What is Covered in this Topic?

This topic looks at...
- how advice and information can be presented
- different techniques to present advice and information
- analysing advice leaflets.

The Purpose of Advice and Information Texts

Advice and information texts can take many forms, but the most common forms that you're likely to come across are leaflets, pamphlets, advice sheets and posters.

The main purpose of these kinds of texts is to give clear information or advice in a brief, quick and interesting way.

As their main purpose is to advise and inform, most texts of this kind contain lots of facts. The way that language is used is very important.

Features of Advice and Information Texts

A variety of techniques can be used to present information clearly and effectively. Here are some of the techniques that are often used:
- headings
- sub-headings
- bullet points
- different fonts
- bold print
- underlining
- colour
- illustrations.

A slogan – an eye-catching phrase that captures the reader's attention – is sometimes used in this kind of writing.

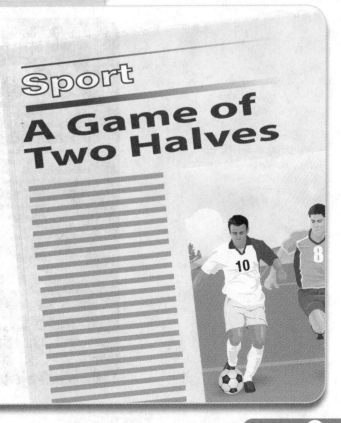

Sport

A Game of Two Halves

Presenting Information

Analysing Advice Leaflets

Now look at this advice card.

💡 *What features are used and what effect do they create?*

The heading is a kind of slogan – it also makes use of a pun – it plays with the well-known expression 'lighten up' and uses it here to mean 'lighten up' up your house by keeping lights on to deter burglars.

Bullet point list to advises on ways to reduce the risk of burglary. Note that this list is quite short and the points give the essential information briefly so that the reader can take in the main points quickly and easily.

Illustrations to show the difference in appearance between the house lit up and the one in darkness linked to the question 'Which home is more attractive to a burglar?'

The use of bold capital letters to emphasise how using lighting can deter burglars.

Advice on how you can find out more information.

Telephone number given in bold, which makes it clear and easy to read.

A series of 'Top Tips' gives advice on how to use lighting to deter burglars. These contain more information about various things that you can do with some specific details, e.g. types of switch, photo-electric cells, as well as the kind of lighting that isn't recommended.

LIGHTEN UP

Which home is more attractive to a burglar?

You can reduce the risk of becoming the victim of a burglary by
- leaving a light on inside the house
- using a timer switch to turn inside lights on
- using outside lighting

USING LIGHTING IN THIS WAY CAN ACT AS A DETERRENT TO BURGLARS

For further Crime Prevention Information please contact the Crime Reduction Officer at your local Police Station.

Tel: 0845 606 0 606

Or refer to the West Yorkshire Police website:

www.westyorkshire.police.uk

Yorkshire & Humber
CRIMESTOPPERS
0800 555 111
Working in partnership with the police

WEST YORKSHIRE POLICE

Strikeback
stinging the criminals!

Card number 7

LIGHTEN UP TOP TIPS

- Leave a light on in more than one well-used room such as the lounge and bedroom, and vary the room you illuminate to avoid predictability

- Use a timer switch to operate the lights as it starts to get dark, especially during autumn and winter, when the days are shorter - frequently change the times that the light comes on so that times do not become predictable

- Outdoor security lighting should operate either on a timer switch or permanently from dusk to dawn - low energy lighting that is controlled by a photo-electric cell (a light sensitive, dusk to dawn switch) is recommended as it is very energy efficient and inexpensive to run - West Yorkshire Police do not recommend the use of movement activated (PIR) lighting

- Outdoor lights, including all wiring should be sited out of reach.

- Privacy for you is also privacy for the burglar to work unseen - keep plants and hedges trimmed and illuminate the dark corners of your premises

Produced by HQ Community Safety

Some advice and information texts only use a few words to put across their message. The words that are used, though, are very carefully chosen to create the effects required.

Look at this example:

The only thing it can't find is itself!

Please remove all belongings from your vehicle when leaving it unoccupied

What advice does it give and how does it put its message across?

The leaflet is advising that car navigation systems (and other valuables) should be removed from cars when the car is left unoccupied.

The large image of the 'sat nav' dominates the leaflet and draws attention to the idea that they are probably the main targets for thieves these days.

The heading 'The only thing it can't find is itself' has a humorous tone to it while at the same time putting across a serious message.

It has a strong visual impact and the clever combination of carefully chosen words and image creates this effect.

Presenting Information

When analysing an advice or information leaflet you need to adopt a structured approach to your analysis. Here is a checklist of things that you could look for and comment on.

Overall impact	Before you start to look at the leaflet in detail, think about your initial impression of it and the effect it has on you.
Heading	What kind of effect does the heading create? Think about the language they use, e.g. puns, a slogan and the presentation (e.g. size and colour). Are sub-headings used?
Content	What kind of information is given? How is language used? You should comment on examples of specific words and phrases and the effects they create when analysing leaflets. Are facts or opinions used? Are questions used?
Presentation	How is the information presented? Look for features such as the use of bullet points, illustrations, tables, boxes, different fonts and colours.

Quick Test

Complete the sentences below.
1. Secondary headings are called

   _____ .

2. Different styles of lettering are called

   _____ .

3. A pun is a play on _____ .

4. A good slogan will capture the reader's

   _____ .

KEY WORDS

Make sure you understand these words before moving on!
- Advice
- Information
- Leaflet
- Pamphlet
- Poster
- Purpose
- Facts
- Language
- Techniques
- Present
- Slogan
- Heading
- Pun
- Illustrations
- Bullet points

Key Words Exercise

Complete the following sentences by finding the missing key words.

1. Things that are true are called ....

2. Advice and information leaflets use a variety of .... to present ideas.

3. A list of ideas can be presented as a series of ....
....

4. Diagrams and .... can be used to help make the information clear.

5. The first thing you read on an advice leaflet is usually the ....

6. Information and advice is often presented in the form of a pamphlet, ...
or ....

7. The main .... of these kinds of texts is to give clear advice
and information.

8. The recommending of a certain kind of action or behaviour is called ....

9. Plays on words are called ....

10. Advice leaflets tell you things and give you lots of ....

11. The purpose of leaflets is to .... information clearly and straightforwardly
and to do this .... needs to be used effectively.

12. A catchy phrase is called a ....

Healthy Eating

You are what you eat!

A good diet is central to overall good health, but which are the best foods to include in your meals, and which ones are best avoided? This section looks at the facts, to help you make realistic, informed choices.

Testing Understanding

Write an analysis of the following advice leaflet, commenting on the following:
- The effects of the heading.
- The content and language.
- The presentation and techniques used.
- The overall effectiveness of the leaflet.

TOP TIPS – for warm weather

- Your dog should always be able to move into a cooler, ventilated environment if he/she is feeling hot.
- Never leave your dog alone in a car. If you want to take your dog with you on a car journey, make sure that your destination is dog-friendly – you won't be able to leave your dog in the car and you don't want your day out to be ruined!
- If you have to leave your dog outside, you must provide a cool, shady spot where he/she can escape from the sun at all times of the day.
- Make sure your dog always has a good supply of drinking water, in a weighted bowl that can't be knocked over. Carry water with you on hot days and give your dog frequent small amounts.
- Never leave your dog in a glass conservatory or a caravan. Even if it is cloudy when you leave, the sun may come out later in the day and make it unbearably hot.
- Groom your dog regularly to get rid of excess hair. Give long-coated breeds a hair-cut at the start of summer, and later in the season, if necessary.
- Dogs need exercise, even when it is hot, but walk your dog early in the morning or later in the evening. Never allow your dog to exercise excessively in hot weather.
- Dogs can get sunburned too – particularly those with light coloured noses or light coloured fur on their ears – ask your vet for advice on pet-safe sunscreen.

ANDREW LINSCOTT/RSPCA PHOTOLIBRARY

COVER PHOTO ANGELA HAMPTON/RSPCA PHOTOLIBRARY

RSPCA

STAY COOL

On a warm day cars heat up like ovens so don't take your dog along for the ride.

°F		°C
90°	32	
86°	3	
82°		
	2	22°
68°	20	20°
64°	18	18°
61°	16	16°

RSPCA, Wilberforce Way, Southwater, Horsham, West Sussex RH13 9RS   Tel: 0300 1234 555
A charity registered in England and Wales. Charity no. 219099
P83 4.09

Printed on 55% recycled paper/ 45% virgin fibre sourced from sustainable forests

LONSDALE

ESSENTIALS

Year 9
KS3 English
Coursebook Answers

Answers

Year 9 KS3 English

Essentials

DESCRIPTIVE WRITING

Page 7
Quick Test
1. verbs 2. sound 3. mood

Page 8
Key Words Exercise

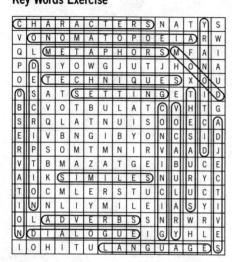

1. dialogue
2. setting; mood
3. characters
4. observation
5. convincing
6. description
7. language
8. thesaurus; dictionary
9. techniques
10. adverbs
11. similes; metaphors
12. adjectives
13. onomatopoeia
14. vocabulary

Page 9
Testing Understanding
1. • Description of Anne's physical appearance, e.g. 'Her eyes were honest and inquiring.'
   • Use of direct speech to capture her voice, e.g. 'I'll do that', she combined dignity with sweetness.'
   • Description of her manner and way of behaving e.g. 'She was graceful'
   • Suggestions of what her character is like underneath, e.g. 'in this young woman there lurked a real firmness.'
   • The use of a simile to describe her hair, e.g. 'round, brown curls, like swallows' nests'
2. • Detailed visual description of the scene.
   • Use of personification ('The water was...stealing away.')
   • Use of adjectives, e.g. smooth, flowing.
   • A sense of peace and quietness created through natural description.

Page 10
Skills Practice
You should have focused closely on the key aspects of each subject for description.

In your writing you should have tried some or all of these techniques:
• Imagery such as similes and metaphors to help your readers re-create your description in their own minds.
• The use of the senses to create a vivid impression of the sights, sounds, tastes, smells and feelings.
• The use of adverbs and adjectives.
• The use of dialogue.
• A range of sentence lengths.

Extension Activity
You should have read your pieces of description clearly and with feeling to make your words come across as effectively as possible. Your partner should have commented on the following:
• Your use of language.
• The techniques you have used to describe your subject.
• Ways that you could improve your description.

You should have made constructive comments about how effective you found your partner's descriptions and given reasons for the points you made. It's likely that comments will focus on the use of language, the use of vocabulary and the effectiveness of imagery, e.g. metaphors and similes. Specific suggestions relating to these would be useful and interesting.

SENTENCES 1

Page 14
Quick Test
1. Four 2. Imperative 3. Phrase 4. Finite

Page 15
Key Words Exercise
1. simple 2. sentence 3. agree 4. finite 5. question 6. action
7. phrase 8. In any order: state; condition 9. exclamation
10. In any order: subject; verb 11. In any order: command; imperative
12. statement

Page 16
Testing Understanding
1. a) Command b) Statement c) Question d) Question
   e) Statement f) Exclamation g) Command h) Exclamation

2.
	Subject	Verb
a)	Joe	ran
b)	Rachael	passed
c)	an evil old witch	sat
d)	Harry and Mario	camped
e)	a large, silver candlestick	stood
f)	Annie	is
g)	Sam	threw
h)	Kim	crossed
i)	the boat	sank
j)	Sandra and Steph	are

3. a) We are going on a long walk tomorrow.
   b) You **are** a good student and work very hard.
   c) I am a keen cyclist.
   d) I thought you **were** going to help me tidy up.
   e) I **was** going to go out tonight but I haven't any money.
   f) My dogs **have** two meals a day.
   g) There **are** lots of people queuing for tickets.
   h) We **were** going to the seaside.

Page 17
Skills Practice
An effective poster should: be attractive and eye-catching; present the information clearly; be easily understood; give clear examples; be designed in a clear and logical way.

Extension Activity
In your presentation you should: explain clearly how you decided to design your poster; why you have used the layout you have; why you used the examples that you have; speak clearly; be prepared to answer questions.

SENTENCES 2

Page 21
Quick Test
1. A group of words that doesn't contain a finite verb and so doesn't make complete sense on its own. 2. To make your writing more varied and interesting. 3. Coordinating conjunction 4. One

Page 22
Key Words Exercise

Complex sentence – A sentence with one main clause and any number of subordinate clauses.

Main clause – A clause that has a finite verb and subject and makes complete sense on its own.

Phrase – A group of words that doesn't contain a finite verb.

Simple sentence – A sentence with just one finite verb.

Coordinating conjunction – Joins two sentences together.

Compound sentence – A sentence made up of two simple sentences.

Multiple sentence – A sentence that contains more than one finite verb.

Subordinate clause – A clause that doesn't make complete sense on its own.

Clause – A group of words with a finite verb.

Page 23
Testing Understanding

1. **Any suitable answers, for example:**
   a) I didn't know about the problem so I can't explain it.
   b) She ran for the bus but she missed it.
   c) Shall we go to the cinema or shall we go bowling?
   d) We must leave now or we will miss the start.
   e) I will tidy up my bedroom but I don't want to.
   f) I will see you tonight and I will pick you up at 7.00pm.

2. a) Sam didn't revise much for his exam and he got a grade C.
      This simply tells you two facts – he didn't revise much and he got a grade C.
      Sam didn't revise much for his exam but he got a grade C.
      This suggests that it is a little surprising that although he didn't revise much he still got a grade C.
   b) We went to drama club and had some hot dogs and pop. This suggests that they had hot dogs and pop at the drama club.
      We went to drama club then had some hot dogs and pop. This suggests that after drama club they went somewhere to have hot dogs and pop.

3. a) swerving round the bend   phrase
   b) I love going on trips   clause
   c) you did well   clause
   d) coming out   phrase
   e) you drive me mad   clause

4. a) I put on my coat (main clause) because it was raining. (subordinate clause)
   b) As the door was locked (subordinate clause) he couldn't get in. (main clause)
   c) Before opening his notebook (subordinate clause) he sharpened his pencil. (main clause)
   d) He was slumped in the chair (main clause) staring vacantly at the television. (subordinate clause)
   e) I paid the bill (main clause) although the food was disgusting. (subordinate clause)

Page 24
Skills Practice

Make sure that your worksheets…
* explain things accurately
* are clear and easy to understand
* give an example of each kind of sentence

* use layout effectively to display information
* contain at least three questions to test understanding
* have an answer sheet.

Extension Activity

You should have discussed how successful you felt the worksheets were in explaining the ideas and how useful you found the questions that were designed to test your understanding. Your discussions should have been constructive. If you had criticisms then you should have supported them with ideas on how the worksheets could be improved.

WRITING FORMAL LETTERS

Page 28
Quick Test

1. The date 2. Yours sincerely 3. When you begin 'Dear Sir' or 'Dear Madam' 4. Top right hand side

Page 29
Key Words Exercise

FORMAL (RALFOM) – When applying for a job your letter of application should be a .... letter.

SINCERELY (NICELYRES) – If you use the person's name you should end your letter 'Yours ....'.

BUSINESS (SUBSINES) – Another term for a formal letter is a .... letter.

DATE (ATED) – You should put the .... under the address.

COMPLAIN (MANICLOP) – If you're not happy with something you might write a letter to ....

ADDRESS (SADREDS) – In the top right hand side you put your ....

APPLICATION (CAPTAINPOIL) – When you apply for a job you usually write a letter of ....

POLITE (PIELOT) – In a letter you should always be ....

PERSUADE (ADRUPEES) – If you want someone to agree with your view you try to .... them.

TONE (ENTO) – Choosing the right words is important to get the right ....

OPINION (INPOINO) – In a letter you might express your own ....

FAITHFULLY (AHFITLYFLU) – If you begin a letter 'Dear Sir' or 'Dear Madam' you should end it 'Yours ....'.

ENQUIRE (QUIREEN) – If you want to find something out you might .... about it.

CONTENT (NOTCENT) – What you write in your letter is called the ....

CONFIRM (MONCRIF) – If you want to make sure you're booked on a holiday you would write to .... the dates and other details.

SALUTATION (ASNAILTOUT) The formal opening part of the letter is known as the ....

Page 30
Testing Understanding
The date is missing. Wrong spellings – unfortunately; there, rang, your, department, they. Sincerely is used instead of faithfully. The tone of the final sentence is wrong – it's too aggressive and threatening.

Page 31
Skills Practice
1. Your letter should…
   • give a clear explanation of the problem
   • give details of when and where you bought the item
   • say what you would expect them to do
   • use a polite and reasonable tone throughout.
2. Your letter should contain these features:
   • The exact dates of your holiday – making sure that your arrival and departure dates are clearly stated.
   • The accommodation that you have booked, e.g. the number of bedrooms, facilities, etc.
   • The number of adults and children that will be arriving.
   • Any other information that you think is important.

Extension Activity
Your poster should have covered the following:
• Correct positioning and layout of addresses
• Date
• Salutation
• Content to suit purpose and audience
• The formal ending (giving alternatives according to salutation).
Your poster should also include between four and six bullet points giving the key points to remember when writing a formal letter.

NOVELS AND SHORT STORIES

Page 35
Quick Test
1. interest 2. to entertain 3. themes 4. plot

Page 36
Key Words Exercise

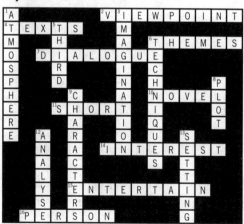

Page 37
Testing Understanding
1. He describes the way they are dressed – the denim trousers and jackets suggest they are workers. Their 'shapeless hats' reinforce this impression.
2. The first man gives the impression of a small but strong character ('strong features') with a sharp intelligent face alert to everything around him ('restless eyes'). We get the impression of a wiry and fit, strong man ('small, strong hands,

slender arms, a thin and bony nose').
3. The second man is the opposite – 'a huge man', 'shapeless of face'. He seems big and slow – 'walked heavily', 'dragging his feet'. Note the animal imagery to describe him – 'the way a bear drags its paws'.
4. The first character is clearly the dominant one. The big man (Lennie) follows the smaller man (George). George tells Lennie not to drink so much – he seems to be looking after Lennie and tries to stop him doing something that might make him ill.
5. George gives Lennie orders and speaks to him like a child. Lennie's answers are very simple and child-like.

Page 38
Skills Practice
Your analysis of each passage should have focused closely on how the writer presents their characters. You should have covered the following:
• The impression you formed of the character.
• The techniques the writer used to create a sense of character.
• How language was used to create effects.

You should have given examples of the language used and the effects created to support the points you made.

Extension Activity
Make sure that you have used plenty of carefully chosen quotations to label your drawing.

PRESENTING INFORMATION

Page 42
Quick Test
1. sub-headings 2. fonts 3. words 4. attention

Page 43
Key Words Exercise
1. facts 2. techniques 3. bullet points 4. illustrations
5. heading 6. **In any order:** leaflet; poster 7. purpose 8. advice
9. puns 10. information 11. present; language 12. slogan

Page 44
Testing Understanding
The heading:
• Large lettering captures attention.
• Use of pale blue highlights key words 'stay' and 'cool'.
• The use of letters shading from white to pale blue suggests a sense of coolness.
• Sub-heading gives factual information, which reinforces the key message.

Content and language:
• Advice given on how to look after a dog in hot weather.
• Bullet points give factual information on making sure your dog is well looked after in hot conditions.

Presentation and effects:
• The effect created by the image of the dog.
• Use of lettering styles and colour to suggest coolness.

Overall effectiveness:
• Assess your response to the leaflet.
• Did you find it effective? Give reasons for your views.

Skills Practice

In your leaflet you should have used...
- headings / sub-headings
- colour and different fonts
- carefully chosen language, e.g. the use of slogans, puns, etc.
- techniques to make your presentation more effective, e.g. the use of bullet points, blocks of text, etc.

Your analysis should give a clear picture of what you wanted to achieve. You should have explained...
- why you chose the heading
- how you decided on the advice / information to include
- the effects you wanted to achieve through language
- the effects you wanted to achieve through presentation

Extension Activity

You should look carefully at the comments on your poster and think about how far you agree with them, making a note of any ways you could improve your poster.

ANALYSING POETRY

Quick Test

1. vocabulary 2. sound 3. In any order: metaphor; simile; personification 4. effects

Key Words Exercise

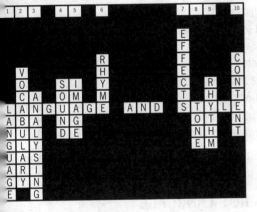

Testing Understanding

There are lots of things you could comment on. Here are some suggestions:

Vocabulary

The vivid descriptions of the blackberries, e.g. 'red', 'green', 'glossy purple', 'stains upon the tongue', 'big, dark blobs', which give a very visual impression of the blackberries while at the same time suggesting taste with 'stains upon the tongue'.

Use of imagery

Similes; 'hard as a knot'; 'sweet like thickened wine'; 'big dark blobs burned / Like a plate of eyes'; 'our palms sticky as Bluebeard's'

Metaphors

'a glossy purple clot'; 'summer's blood'; 'inked up'

Tone

The tone in the first section is one of excitement and gives a strong impression of the eagerness to collect as many blackberries as possible. The tone changes in the second section of the poem to one of disappointment as the blackberries rot. This contrasts to the feeling in the first part of the poem.

Skills Practice

Make sure that you choose your poem carefully. Choose one that you have plenty to say about. Use your notes as the basis of your analysis. Make sure that you have covered the following:
- What you think the poem is about.
- The use of vocabulary and imagery.
- The tone and atmosphere created (and how).
- The use of effects such as alliteration, onomatopoeia, etc.

Remember that you should have used individual words or short quotations from the poem to illustrate your ideas.

Extension Activity

You should plan your talk carefully so that you know what you're going to say. When giving your talk make sure that you don't read out from your notes though. If you need prompts you could write key ideas on cards to remind you of the order of your points and help you stick to your plan.

WRITING FROM DIFFERENT CULTURES

Quick Test

1. non-standard English 2. world 3. ritual 4. voice

Key Words Exercise

VOCABULARY –	The words or language used.
CULTURE –	The customs, way of life, traditions, etc. of a particular group of people.
RITUALS –	These are often carried out at religious ceremonies.
CUSTOMS –	The usual ways of behaving or doing things.
NON-STANDARD –	Dialect is a _____ form of English.
VOICE –	Non-standard English can be used in writing to create a sense of _____.
TRADITION –	A custom, belief or way of doing things, handed down from generation to generation.
BELIEFS –	A person's or group's religious ideas.
WORLD –	Literature from different cultures can come from all over the _____.
DIALECT –	The form of speech of a particular region or part of the world.
METAPHOR –	A kind of imagery where one thing is said to be another.
SIMILE –	A comparison where one thing is said to be like another.

Testing Understanding

Here are some ideas that you might have noted:
1. The Butterfly represents the 'higher life' – living a good and sin-free life. Butterflies fly free in the heavens whilst caterpillars crawl on leaves or the ground.
2. They don't take him seriously and find it hard not to laugh. At the end, however, the speaker realises that the preacher was right and it is better to be a butterfly than a caterpillar.
3. He is the only one who can keep a straight face.
4. The food indicates a different culture with its references to things we are not familiar with, e.g. fufu and pigtail.
5. The spelling of caterpillar (kyatta-pilla); the lines 'That was de life preacher' / 'And you was right'.

Page 59

Skills Practice

You should have commented on the following:

- What the title of the poem suggests to you. The title of the poem can give you important clues about the poem itself (e.g. as in 'Be a Butterfly').
- What the poem is about. Try to be clear in your own mind what the poem is about – what is happening, what kind of message the poet wants to give you.
- Whether the poet uses dialect or non-standard English. If so, you should have thought about the effect that it has on the poem – its effect is going to be very important.
- Whether the poet uses imagery (e.g. metaphors, similes, etc.). If so, you should have given examples and commented on the effects created.
- What effects are created by the language used. You should have looked at individual words and phrases that strike you as being important and explained why.
- Whether the poet creates an impression of the culture / traditions / beliefs, etc. If so, you should have commented on how they were presented and what effects you think they have on the poem.
- What you feel about the poem overall. You should have tried to give reasons for why you feel the way you do about the poem.

Extension Activity

Experiment with different ways of reading the poem and think about any differences or effects that you can create through your readings. Make sure that you talk to your partner and share your ideas.

MEDIA TEXTS – ADVERTISEMENTS

Page 63

Quick Test

1. To persuade people to do / feel something. **2.** A command.

3. To add emphasis to a word or idea.

4. To build a positive description.

Page 64

Key Words Exercise

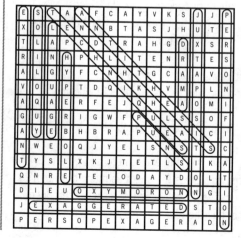

Page 65

Testing Understanding

1. Bisto gravy.
2. Probably mothers (perhaps fathers) – whoever cooks the evening meal in the house.
3. The striking and unusual heading, 'Forget the TV news' captures the reader's attention. The sub-heading changes the

focus – 'Your family's news' suggests it's good to eat together and talk to each other as a family. The 'chicken pie and gravy' creates a homely, comforting and tasty image.

4. The design is the Bisto logo, but it usually says 'Aah! Bisto'. The variation suggests Wednesday night, as mid-week, is a good time to sit down and eat together as a family.
5. The company name only appears in the web address given at the bottom of the advert.
6. The smaller print at the bottom draws attention to a scheme where you get some kind of reward. The lack of further details might encourage you to visit the website to see what it's about. Note the emphasis of 'family' here again.
7. The answer to this is your own personal response. Whatever your views are, make sure that you explain your comments and support them with specific references to the advert.

Page 66

Skills Practice

Make sure that you've commented on the following:

- The heading / slogan and sub-headings.
- The effects created by photos / pictures / designs, etc.
- The information given and how language is used.
- The overall effect that the adverts have on you.
- Think about the level of detail needed to answer the questions on the Bisto advert to help you approach your adverts.

Extension Activity

Make sure that you have thought about these points carefully:

- Your slogan or heading.
- The images you've used.
- The text you've used – why have you used certain words / phrases?
- What techniques you've used to catch your reader's attention and make your advert persuasive. Did you include techniques such as alliteration and repetition? How did you make your advert persuasive – did you use clever adjectives or imperatives, or was it more to do with the images?

Your written explanation of your advert should be quite detailed. You should have made a note of your partner's response to your advert.

SHAKESPEARE'S LANGUAGE

Page 70

Quick Test

1. pun **2.** hyperbole **3.** alone **4.** juxtaposition

Page 71

Key Words Exercise

1. exaggerated; extravagant
2. drama
3. juxtaposition
4. techniques
5. personification
6. soliloquy
7. hyperbole
8. oxymoron
9. language
10. puns
11. antithesis

Testing Understanding

1. Shakespeare uses antithesis in love / hate and love / loathe. The use of this antithesis emphasises the problem facing Juliet and the love she feels for Romeo even though, as a Montague, she should hate him.

2. An oxymoron is used in 'brawling love'. Love is making Romeo sad because he loves Rosaline, but she is indifferent to him.

3. a) The pun is on the word 'steal', which means 'to go secretly' and 'to rob', i.e. take things that are not his.

   b) Claudius calls Hamlet son (even though he isn't his son) and Hamlet uses the word 'sun' (meaning that Claudius is watching him too closely). There's also a play on 'kin' (relative) and 'kind' (being nice to him).

   c) The pun is on the word 'light', which is referring to the torch or candle that Othello carries and light also meaning Desdemona's life.

Skills Practice

1. When you have identified your examples of antithesis or oxymoron make sure that you explain carefully what words are used to create the antithesis or oxymoron and explain the effects created.

   Example answer: in *Macbeth*, Shakespeare uses antithesis to create a vivid sense of the way things are slipping from good into evil:

   'Good things of day begin to droop and drowse,
   While night's black agents their preys do rouse.'
   (Act 3 Scene 2 lines 52–53)

   Here the idea of 'good things' and 'black agents' are set in opposition to each other with the link between 'black' and evil created. The idea of good things beginning to 'droop and drowse' gives the impression that good is in decline and the evil is gaining strength.

2. **You should have explained what is being personified and the effects created.**

   Example answer: In *Hamlet*, the dawn is described in this way:
   'But look the morn in russet mantle clad
   Walks o'er the dew of yon high eastward hill.'
   Here the dawn is described as if it were a person dressed in the golden brown that is the colour of dawn walking over a high hill to the east (where the sun rises). This creates a vivid picture in the mind of the dawn beginning to break and adds a sense of peace to the scene.

3. **You should have explained how the puns work and how the effects are created.**

   Example answer: In *Hamlet*, Hamlet has a conversation with a grave digger (described as a clown here) about whose grave he is digging.

   Hamlet: ...Whose grave's this, sirrah?
   First Clown: Mine, sir.
                  [sings]
                  O, a pit of clay for to be made
                  For such a guest is meet.
   Hamlet: I think it be thine, indeed; for thou liest in't.
   First Clown: You lie out on't, sir, and therefore it is not yours: for my part, I do not lie in't, and yet it is mine.
   Hamlet: Thou dost lie in't, to be in't and say it is thine:

'tis for the dead, not for the quick; therefore thou liest.

The pun here is all based around the word 'lie' – meaning to lie down or lie in the grave but also meaning to tell an untruth. The word play here creates a moment of humour at a particularly tense moment in the play.

4. In your short essay you might have commented on some of these ideas:
   - The use of imagery, e.g. metaphors, similes, personification.
   - The use of vocabulary, e.g. commenting on the ideas that individual words or phrases have brought to your mind.
   - The use of antithesis.
   - The use of hyperbole.

Extension Activity

Think carefully about the effects that you want your examples to create. Discuss the effects with your partner before writing your explanations.

READING FOR MEANING

Quick Test

1. What information you need. 2. Making brief notes directly on a copy of your text. 3. understanding 4. key points

Key Words Exercise

1. comprehension 2. extensive reading 3. skimming 4. information 5. annotation 6. summary 7. highlighting 8. notes 9. intensive reading 10. purpose 11. key points 12. scanning

Testing Understanding

1. a) Three b) Stones c) They sometimes blew down in strong winds
2. Canvas hats coated with tar, leather aprons and cowhide boots
3. Basic food and not a lot of it.
4. Chebaccos; thirty feet
5. Because it was poor-quality fish that wasn't worth selling. The best fish was brought back to port to sell.
6. Fishing with a line and hooks. When a fish is caught the line is pulled up by hand.
7. Because they were large muscular men.
8. By how many fish they caught.
9. To keep a check on how many fish each man had caught.
10. By drying it or later ice was used.

Skills Practice

Make sure that you have...
- selected your passage carefully making sure that it has the right kind of material to ask a variety of questions on.
- thought about your questions carefully and made sure that they can be answered by reading the passage; remember, your questions are to test understanding of the passage and not general knowledge
- been careful about how you have phrased your questions – make sure that it is clear exactly what it is you're asking
- created a variety of question types.

Extension Activity

Remember to be constructive in your discussion and make suggestions on how questions could be improved if you feel they could be. Make notes on your discussion points as you go along and write up the key points at the end.

PUNCTUATION

Page 84
Quick Test
1. possessive 2. contractions 3. homophones

Page 85
Key Words Exercise

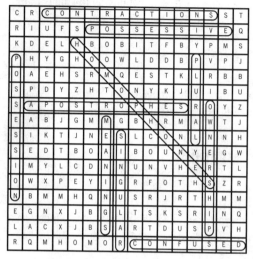

1. plural
2. ownership
3. possession
4. contractions
5. singular
6. homophones
7. confused
8. possessive
9. meanings
10. apostrophes

Page 86
Testing Understanding
1
  a) I know **it's** raining and the forecast says **it's** going to get worse.
  b) The car has just had **its** annual service so, with a bit of luck, **it's** going to get us to Cornwall without a problem.
  c) The way that dog is baring **its** teeth and snarling, I think **it's** going to turn nasty.
  d) **It's** always been an ambition of mine to become a film star but I don't think **it's** going to happen.
  e) The eagle swooped down onto **its** prey, grabbed it in **its** talons and flew back to **its** nest.

2. a) **They're** coming to stay this weekend and **they're** bringing **their** nephew with them.
  b) I went **there** last year and saw **their** carnival procession bu~~t~~ I've heard **they're** not having one this year.
  c) **Who's** coming with me to see **their** performance and **whose** car are we going in?
  d) If **you're** short of money again **you're** going to have to use **your** savings.
  e) If you've lost **your** book **you're** not going to borrow mine.

3. a) The car's headlights were not very bright and the road's twists and turns made driving difficult. (Cars' would also be accepted.)
  b) The boys' changing room was very noisy and the teacher's voice could hardly be heard.
  c) The young child's painting won the competition and was displayed in the town's art gallery.
  d) The sun's rays shone through the window and the old lady's eyes were dazzled for a moment.
  e) I'm going to the doctor's tomorrow so I'll get a prescription then.

Page 87
Skills Practice
Make sure that...
- one information sheet covers contraction apostrophes
- one information sheet covers commonly confused words
- one information sheet covers possessive apostrophes.

It's important that your information sheets present the information both effectively and accurately. Check your understanding of the material in the chapter very carefully.

Extension Activity
Your worksheets should give good practice of the ideas contained in your information sheets. An important part of the activity here is looking at your partner's information sheets and doing the worksheets, and discussing your thoughts about their material. Equally important is hearing what your partner has to say about your work.

ACKNOWLEDGEMENTS

The author and publisher are grateful to the copyright holders for permission to use quoted materials and images.

Every effort has been made to trace copyright holders and obtain their permission for the use of copyright material. The authors and publishers will gladly receive information enabling them to rectify any error or omission in subsequent editions. All facts are correct at time of going to press.

Lonsdale
4 Grosvenor Place
London SW1X 7DL

School orders: 015395 64910
School enquiries: 015395 65921
Email: enquiries@lettsandlonsdale.co.uk
Website: www.lettsandlonsdale.com

ISBN: 978-1-906491-30-7

01/060709

Published by Lonsdale, a division of Huveaux PLC

© 2009 Lonsdale.

British Library Cataloguing in Publication Data.

A CIP record of this book is available from the British Library.

Book Concept and Development: Helen Jacobs
Commissioning Editor: Rebecca Skinner
Author: Steven Croft
Project Editors: Michelle I'Anson and Charlotte Christensen
Cover Design: Angela English
Inside Concept Design: Helen Jacobs and Sarah Duxbury
Text Design and Layout: Ian Wrigley
Artwork: Letts and Lonsdale

Printed in Italy

Lonsdale makes every effort to ensure that all paper used in our books is made from wood pulp obtained from well-managed forests, controlled sources and recycled wood or fibre.

Design your own advice / information poster on a topic of your choice.

Think carefully about the following when designing your poster:
* Your use of headings / sub-headings.
* Your use of language.
* Your use of techniques to make your presentation more effective.

When you have finished your poster write an analysis of it explaining what overall effects you wanted to achieve and what decisions you made when designing it.

You should explain…
* why you chose the heading
* how you decided on the advice / information to include
* the effects you wanted to achieve through language
* the effects you wanted to achieve through presentation.

Extension Activity

Design a short questionnaire asking for views on how well your poster put across the advice / information. Ask three or four other people to look at your poster and fill in your questionnaire, and then examine the results carefully to see if you think there is any way you could improve your poster.

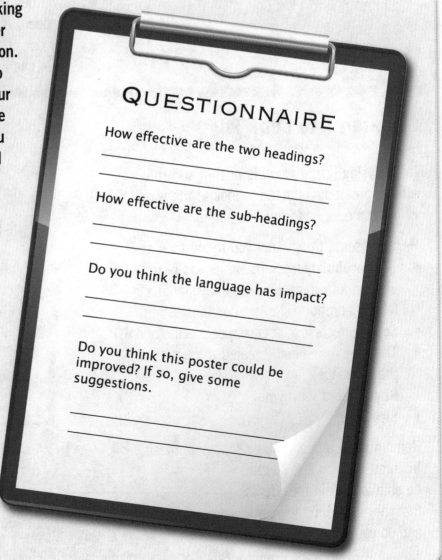

QUESTIONNAIRE

How effective are the two headings?
_____
_____

How effective are the sub-headings?
_____
_____

Do you think the language has impact?
_____
_____

Do you think this poster could be improved? If so, give some suggestions.
_____
_____

Analysing Poetry

What is Covered in this Topic?

This topic looks at...
- how to approach a poem
- features to look for
- studying a twentieth Century poem
- studying a pre-twentieth Century poem.

Approaching a Poem

When studying a poem the first thing you should do is read it carefully several times and form a general understanding of what it's about (the poem's meaning).

Then ask yourself three questions:
1. What is the poem about? (The content and meaning of the poem.)
2. How does the poet use language? (The style the poem is written in.)
3. Why does the poet use language in that way? (The effects created by the poem.)

Features to Look For

In analysing how a poem is written and the effects created, you need to look at the way in which the poet has used language.

Here are some things that you might look at:
- The vocabulary (specific words and phrases).
- The use of imagery i.e. figurative language (e.g. metaphors, similes, personification).
- Sound effects (e.g. onomatopoeia, alliteration).
- The tone and mood (created through the language).
- Rhythm and / or rhyme.
- Structure.

Remember, you need to be able to spot these features, but you also need to be able to explain the effects that they create in the poem and on you – the reader.

Analysing a Twentieth Century Poem

Poetry deals with all kinds of themes and ideas but they are often linked to the times in which they were written and the kind of world in which the poet lives.

In this poem the poet, Carol Ann Duffy, imagines a war photographer developing his photographs, remembering all the horrors he has seen.

As he develops one of his photographs the face of the victim begins to form and the memory of the suffering of this moment comes flooding back to him.

Read the poems carefully.

💡 *What effects are created by the highlighted images in the poem below? What are your overall feelings about the poem?*

War Photographer by Carol Ann Duffy

In his darkroom he is finally alone
with spools of suffering set out in ordered rows.
The only light is red and softly glows,
as though this were a church and he
a priest preparing to intone a Mass.
Belfast. Beirut. Phnom Penh. All flesh is grass.

He has a job to do. Solutions slop in trays
beneath his hands which did not tremble then
though seem to now. Rural England. Home again
to ordinary pain which simple weather can dispel,
to fields which don't explode beneath the feet
of running children in a nightmare heat.

Something is happening. A stranger's features
faintly start to twist before his eyes,
a half-formed ghost. He remembers the cries
of this man's wife, how he sought approval
without words to do what someone must
and how the blood stained into foreign dust.

A hundred agonies in black-and-white
from which his editor will pick out five or six
for Sunday's supplement. The reader's eyeballs prick
with tears between the bath and pre-lunch beers.
From the aeroplane he stares impassively at where
he earns his living and they do not care.

Annotations (left):

The film is on spools but contains the undeveloped photographs of the suffering of the many people he photographed.

Back to the safety of England – a contrast to the land he has returned from where children running in the fields can be blown up by land mines.

The hundreds of photos he has taken showing the suffering caused by war.

Annotations (right):

The developing is a solemn process as it will reveal images of suffering.

A man's image begins to form as the photo is developed – twisted with pain and suffering, a half-formed ghost because the image hasn't fully formed yet but also a ghost because the man is probably dead now.

When the pictures appear in the Sunday paper the reader is momentarily moved but then forgets it as they go for a bath and a pre-lunch beer.

Analysing Poetry

Analysing a Pre-Twentieth Century Poem

Thomas Hardy's poem is also about war but from an earlier time. Drummer Hodge is a young British army drummer boy who died in South Africa during the Boer War (1899–1903). Drummer boys were often about 11 or 12 years old.

Read the poem carefully and think about these ideas:

- How Drummer Hodge is buried.
- How Hardy gives a sense that he is far from home.
- The tone of the poem.
- What effect you think Hardy might have wanted it to have on the reader.

You might have noted the following:

- There is no dignity or ceremony about his burial. He is simply thrown into the grave 'Uncoffined', just as he was found.
- Hardy uses South African words such as 'kopje-crest', (a small hill), veldt (open grassland plains), and mentions the 'foreign constellations' (the star constellations are different in the southern hemisphere).
- The tone of the poem is sad and regretful and emphasises the futility and waste of life that is one of the consequences of war.

Drummer Hodge by Thomas Hardy

They throw in Drummer Hodge, to rest
    Uncoffined – just as found:
His landmark is a kopje-crest
    That breaks the veldt around;
And foreign constellations west
    Each night above his mound.

Young Hodge the drummer never knew –
    Fresh from his Wessex home –
The meaning of the broad Karoo,
    The Bush, the dusty loam,
And why uprose to nightly view
    Strange stars amid the gloam.

Yet portion of that unknown plain
    Will Hodge for ever be;
His homely Northern breast and brain
    Grow to some Southern tree,
And strange-eyed constellations reign
    His stars eternally.

An Earlier Pre-Twentieth Century Poem

When reading *Drummer Hodge* you probably didn't notice many differences in terms of vocabulary between that poem and a poem that might have been written more recently. In some pre-twentieth century poems, though, the differences are more noticeable.

Look at this poem written by Ben Jonson, a poet and dramatist, after the death of his first son, Benjamin, who died at the age of seven.

💡 *What do you notice about the language?*

On my first Sonne by Ben Jonson

Farewell, thou child of my right hand, and joy;
My sinne was too much hope of thee, lov'd boy,
Seven yeeres tho'wert lent to me, and I thee pay,
Exacted by thy fate, on the just day.
O, could I loose all father, now. For why
Will man lament the state he should envie?
To have so soone scap'd worlds, and fleshes rage,
And, if no other miserie, yet age?
Rest in soft peace, and, ask'd, say here doth lye
Ben. Jonson his best piece of poetrie.
For whose sake, hence-forth, all his vowes be such,
As what he loves may never like too much.

You will have noticed the following:

- The spelling is quite different from modern spelling (although we can still understand the words).
- Some words have apostrophes in them where we wouldn't normally use an apostrophe today.
- Some words are ones that we don't use nowadays, e.g. 'wert' meaning 'was' and 'tho' which is an abbreviation of 'thou', meaning 'you'.

When reading pre-twentieth Century poetry you might find...

- old fashioned words that we don't use nowadays
- the word order is different from the modern word order we would use
- ideas that relate to the particular historical time it was written in
- references that you might need to look up to fully understand what they mean
- spellings that differ from modern English.

Quick Test

1. The words in a poem are called the _____.
2. Onomatopoeia and alliteration create _____ effects in a poem.
3. Name three kinds of imagery (figurative language).
4. When analysing a poem you need to explain the _____ created by the language.

KEY WORDS

Make sure you understand these words before moving on!

- Content
- Language
- Style
- Effects
- Analysing
- Vocabulary
- Imagery
- Sound
- Tone
- Mood
- Rhythm
- Rhyme

Analysing Poetry

Solve the clues to complete the quiz word and spell out the key words across the middle.

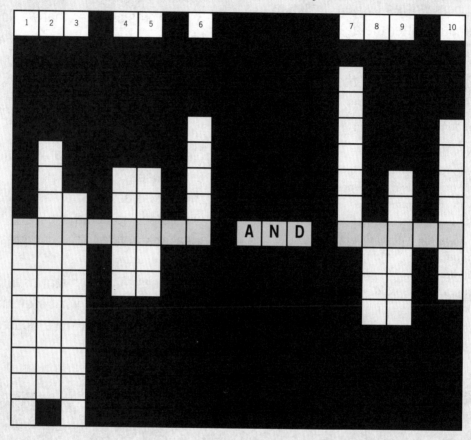

1. Poets choose the _____ they use very carefully when writing a poem.

2. The words they use.

3. You do this when you examine a poem carefully looking at the effects the language creates.

4. Onomatopoeia can be used to create a _____ effect.

5. A simile is an example of an _____.

6. Lines that end in a similar sound do this.

7. You need to explain the _____ created by the features you identify.

8. A voice might have a particular _____.

9. The 'beat' of a poem.

10. The idea in a poem.

Testing Understanding

Read this poem carefully and write an analysis of it.

Remember to ask yourself the following:
- What the poem is about (meaning).
- How the poet uses language.
- Why the poet uses language in that way.

Comment on these features, explaining the effects that are created:
- vocabulary
- use of imagery
- tone.

Blackberry-Picking by Seamus Heaney

Late August, given heavy rain and sun
For a full week, the blackberries would ripen.
At first, just one, a glossy purple clot
Among others, red, green, hard as a knot.
You ate that first one and its flesh was sweet
Like thickened wine: summer's blood was in it
Leaving stains upon the tongue and lust for
Picking. Then red ones inked up and that hunger
Sent us out with milk-cans, pea-tins, jam-pots
Where briars scratched and wet grass bleached our boots.
Round hayfields, cornfields and potato-drills
We trekked and picked until the cans were full,
Until the tinkling bottom had been covered
With green ones, and on top big dark blobs burned
Like a plate of eyes. Our hands were peppered
With thorn pricks, our palms sticky as Bluebeard's.

We hoarded the fresh berries in the byre.
But when the bath was filled we found a fur,
A rat-grey fungus, glutting on our cache.
The juice was stinking too. Once off the bush
The fruit fermented, the sweet flesh would turn sour.
I always felt like crying. It wasn't fair
That all the lovely canfuls smelt of rot.
Each year I hoped they'd keep, knew they would not.

Analysing Poetry

Choose a poem of your own and write an analysis of it.

Use the following approach:
- Read the poem through carefully several times.
- Make a note of the ideas that come into your head to begin with.
- Write down what you think the poem is about.
- Make notes on how the poet uses language (e.g. vocabulary, metaphors, similes) and the effects that they create.
- Describe the kind of tone and / or atmosphere created.
- Make a note of other effects created in the poem (e.g. rhyme, rhythm, alliteration, onomatopoeia).
- Note your overall thoughts and feelings about the poem.
- Use your notes to write up your analysis remembering to quote specific examples to illustrate your ideas.

Extension Activity

Use your completed analysis to prepare a talk to give to your class about your poem.

Plan what you're going to say carefully – don't just read out your analysis.

Structure your talk so that you give your audience a clear idea about what your chosen poem is about.

End your talk by saying why you chose this poem and what you find interesting or enjoyable about it. Allow time for your audience to ask you questions about it at the end.

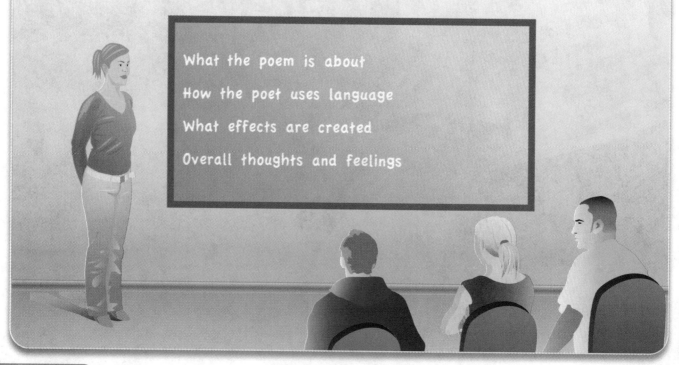

What the poem is about

How the poet uses language

What effects are created

Overall thoughts and feelings

Writing From Different Cultures

What is Covered in this Topic?

This topic looks at...
- poetry from different cultures
- prose from different cultures
- how language is used.

Different Cultures and Traditions

Writing can come from a wide range of different **cultures**, each with their own distinctive **traditions** and ways of life.

How many examples of literature from different places in the **world** have you read?

Here are some broad areas:

Even within each of these broad areas there are many different kinds of cultures and traditions, each with their own distinctive **ways of life**. This is reflected in their writings.

Europe

USA

Asia

Different Cultures and Traditions

Africa

South America

Australia

How Writings Differ

From what you've read from writings from other cultures, you might have noticed the following:
- Different traditions, **customs**, **beliefs**, **rituals** and ways of life are described.

- Unfamiliar words are used to describe particular things.
- **Non-standard** or **dialect** forms are sometimes used to reflect the **voice** of the speaker or writer.

Writing From Different Cultures

Poetry From Different Cultures

Read the following poem carefully and think about...
- what the poet describes
- what kind of atmosphere she creates
- how she uses language.

Blessing by Imtiaz Dharker

The skin cracks like a pod.
There never is enough water.

Imagine the drip of it,
the small splash, echo
in a tin mug,
the voice of a kindly god.

Sometimes, the sudden rush
of fortune. The municipal pipe bursts,
silver crashes to the ground
and the flow has found
a roar of tongues. From the huts,
a congregation: every man woman
child for streets around
butts in, with pots,
brass, copper, aluminium,
plastic buckets,
frantic hands,

and naked children
screaming in the liquid sun,
their highlights polished to perfection,
flashing light,
as the blessing sings
over their small bones.

Here are some ideas you might have noted about the poem:
- The poem describes the bursting of a water pipe in a village where water is very scarce and how the people respond to this event.
- The atmosphere the poet creates is one of great excitement as everyone rushes to catch as much water as they can in any kind of container they can find.
- The dry, drought conditions are captured vividly through the use of a **simile** – 'The skin cracks like a pod'.
- **Metaphors** are used to create a vivid impression of the scene, e.g. 'the sudden rush of fortune', 'silver crashes to the ground', 'liquid sun'.
- **Vocabulary** is used to create the sense of excitement, e.g. 'roar of tongues', 'frantic hands', 'children screaming'.

Prose From Different Cultures

The following extract from *Green Days By The River* by Michael Anthony is set in Trinidad. Read through it carefully.

💡 *What do you notice about the vocabulary that the writer uses?*

The description contains several words that you're probably not familiar with but which are commonly used terms in Trinidadian culture. You might have noted these terms:

- Sapodillas, shaddocks, star-apples and pomerac, which are all kinds of fruit that are found in Trinidad.
- Roti – a kind of bread commonly baked in the West Indies.
- Creole – from a mixture of European and another culture.
- 'Ortoire' – the name of the river.

You will have also noticed how the writer describes activities, which are typical of life in that part of the world and that culture, e.g. fruit picking and rice cutting.

MR GIDHAREE let me climb some other fruit trees and we collected some fruit in an old sack he had. I picked sapodillas, shaddocks, and star-apples, and he showed me where the banana trees were. These had huge bunches of ripe bananas and here was where the birds feasted. Most of the bunches were rotting and fly-infested and the bananas themselves were half-eaten by birds.

'You want?' he said.

'No. Don't really feel like it so much. But I smelling pomerac.'

He smiled and looked up. 'You nose good, boy.'

In the tangle of branches above the banana trees were clusters of the red, pear-shaped fruit we called pomerac, and finding the tree now, I climbed and picked a good deal. When I came down again, he said, 'Okay. What you pick is for you – for when you going home'

'You don't want none?' I wished he would take some, at least.

'Just a couple for Rosie, that's all.'

I took out some nice ones and put them aside then I pulled up one of the vines on the ground and tied the sack-mouth. Then I took the sack into our little hut and I came back and took Rosalie's fruit into the hut. Tiger, the spotted dog, woke up when I went in the second time, and at once he pricked up his ears and was on the alert.

'Tiger:' I said, 'lazy!' I approached him cautiously. Somehow I was still afraid of this one.

He looked up at me with soft eyes. Then he wagged his tail a little. I went out again, and Mr Gidharee said, 'Listen, we going down by the rice now.'

'All right.'

'When you feel peckish, say. We have plenty roti in the bag.' I said nothing.

He looked at me as if doubtful. 'You ain't one of those *creole* who shame to eat roti!'

'Me? No, Mr Gidharee. Not me.'

'Oho,' he said.

We cut rice paddies for about two hours steadily, working in the part of the field near the river. The sun was hot now, and Ortoire, like a long, slithering snake, eased beside us. We were using grass-knives, and after Mr Gidharee had shown me what to do, I did not need any more showing and we cut rice man for man.

Writing From Different Cultures

Approaching Writing From Different Cultures

In addition to the language used and the effects created, there are other features you can look for in writing.

Here are some ideas:

- Attitudes
- Vocabulary of the culture / tradition
- Environment / living conditions
- **Cultural features**
- Cultural differences / similarities
- Beliefs / religion
- Descriptions of places

Quick Test

Complete the sentences below.

1. Another word for dialect form is

_____ .

2. Literature from different cultures can come from anywhere in the _____ .

3. Another word for a ceremony is a

_____ .

4. A writer sometimes uses non-standard forms of English to reflect the speaker's

_____ .

Key Words Exercise

Unscramble the anagrams to find the key words, then draw a line to match them to the right definition.

CAROVALBUY

RUTCLUE

SAILRUT

CUTMOSS

RANDSANDNOT

COVIE

RADIOTINT

FIBEELS

DOLWR

CITADEL

EARTHMOP

MILEIS

A person's or group's religious ideas.

A kind of imagery where one thing is said to be another.

The words or language used.

The customs, way of life, traditions, etc., of a particular group of people.

The form of speech of a particular region or part of the world.

Literature from different cultures can come from all over the _____.

These are often carried out at religious ceremonies.

Dialect is a _____ form of English.

A comparison where one thing is said to be like another.

A custom, belief or way of doing things, handed down from generation to generation.

Non-standard English can be used in writing to create a sense of _____.

The usual ways of behaving or doing things.

Writing From Different Cultures

Testing Understanding

Be a Butterfly by Grace Nichols

Don't be a kyatta-pilla
Be a butterfly
old preacher screamed
to illustrate his sermon
of Jesus and the higher life

rivulets of well-earned
sweat sliding down
his muscly mahogany face
in the half-empty school church
we sat shaking with muffling
laughter
watching our mother trying to save
herself from joining the wave

only our father remaining poker face
and afterwards we always went home to
split peas Sunday soup
with dumplings, fufu* and pigtail*

Don't be a kyatta-pilla
Be a butterfly
Be a butterfly

That was de life preacher
and you was right.

* fufu – dough made with corn meal
* pigtail – salted, cured pig's tail

Read this poem carefully and answer these questions.

1. What does the Butterfly represent to the preacher in the first stanza?
2. How does the speaker and most of the congregation respond to the preacher's sermon? How does the speaker feel at the end of the poem?
3. How does the father react?
4. What does the description of the Sunday lunch tell you?
5. Can you find any examples of non-standard English?

Look at some other poems from different cultures and pick one for more detailed study.

You will find your school's resource learning centre or library useful in finding examples of poetry from other cultures. Or you may have anthologies in the classroom that you can use.

When you have chosen your poem make notes on it using these questions as a checklist:
- What does the title of the poem suggest to you?
- What is the poem about?
- Does the poet use dialect or non-standard English?
- Does the poet use imagery (e.g. metaphors, similes, etc.)?
- What effects are created by the language used?
- Does the poet create an impression of the culture / traditions / beliefs, etc? If so, how are they presented and what effects do you think they have on the poem?
- What do you feel about the poem overall?

When you have completed all your notes, write them up as a full analysis of the poem.

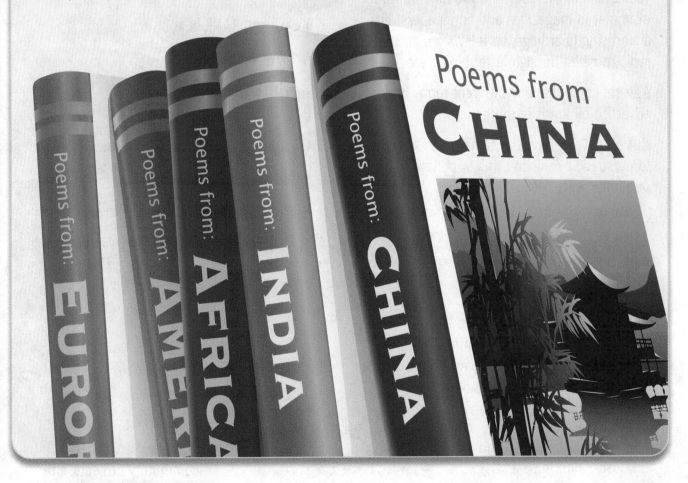

Extension Activity

Work with a partner to take turns to read your poems aloud to each other (you could try recording your readings and listening to them several times).

Talk about your responses to each other's readings. Does reading the poems aloud change your ideas about them in any way?

Media Texts – Advertisements

What is Covered in this Topic?

This topic looks at...
- different types of advertisements
- the features of advertisements
- the language of advertisements
- analysing advertisements.

The Purpose of Advertising

Advertisements will be very familiar to you – you see them everyday. They're all around, for example, in magazines and newspapers, on advertising hoardings, on television, on the radio, pushed through letter boxes, etc.

Adverts come in many different forms and advertise all kinds of things.

But all adverts have the same broad purpose: to persuade people to think or behave in a particular way.

SAVINGS BANK
Watch your money grow with our new rate of
5.7%

SALE NOW ON
up to 50% off

Lonsdale News
Olympic Games: Report Claim

Types of Advertising

Here are some of the many things that are advertised. You'll probably have seen examples of them all at one time or another.

Products, e.g. computers, food and drink, holidays, clothes and furniture.

Services, e.g. finance and loans, plumbing and gardening.

Public Services, e.g. community projects, fire safety and health.

Advertising

Careers, e.g. as a driving instructor, teacher or nurse

Political, e.g. political parties and local councils.

Charities, e.g. the RSPCA, Help the Aged and Oxfam.

Features of Advertisements

Although all adverts are different, many of them use the same techniques and have certain features in common.

Here are some features / techniques you might have noticed:

- Headings and slogans – these are the key words that catch people's attention and make them want to look at the advert and read it. The people who created the advert will have spent a lot of time making sure the advert is both eye-catching and persuasive.

- Appeal – all adverts are designed to appeal to something that you want or need, for example, comfort, excitement, fashion, money, or a sense of conscience.
- Language – some adverts contain very few words and rely on photographs or images to create their effects. Some just use a catchy slogan. But many use various language techniques, such as alliteration or rhyme, to make their point.

An Example of an Advert

The advert shown here for Eternity rings has the following features:

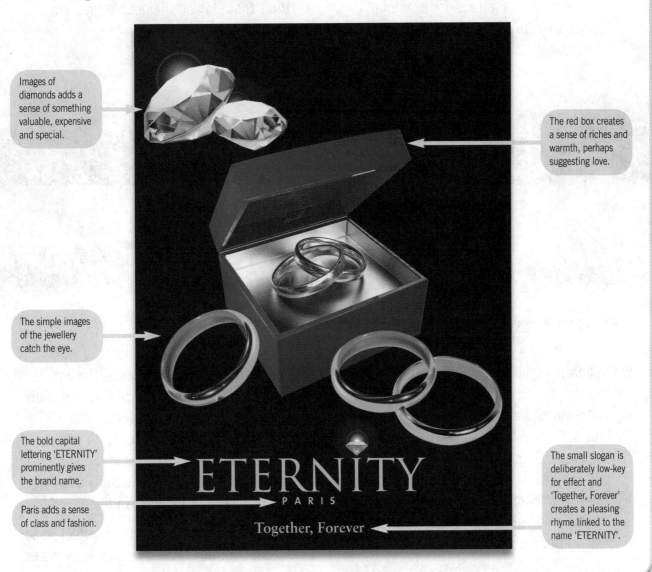

Images of diamonds adds a sense of something valuable, expensive and special.

The red box creates a sense of riches and warmth, perhaps suggesting love.

The simple images of the jewellery catch the eye.

The bold capital lettering 'ETERNITY' prominently gives the brand name.

Paris adds a sense of class and fashion.

The small slogan is deliberately low-key for effect and 'Together, Forever' creates a pleasing rhyme linked to the name 'ETERNITY'.

ETERNITY
PARIS
Together, Forever

Media Texts – Advertisements

Language in Advertisements

Here are some of the language techniques that are often used in adverts:

- **Exaggeration** – words are used that give the best possible impression of the **product**; exaggeration is often used to achieve this, for example, 'The most fantastic offer!'.
- Use of **imperatives** – verbs that command you to do something, for example, 'Buy now!'.
- Claims that can't be proved – for example, 'You can't afford to miss this offer!'.
- Appealing words, often **adjectives** – descriptive words that draw in the reader and create a vivid effect, for example, 'beautiful', 'luxurious', 'exclusive', 'delicious', 'tasty', 'stylish'.

- **Repetition** – important or striking words are repeated for emphasis.
- Sound appeal – the use of alliteration, assonance or rhyme to create effects, for example, e.g. 'soft, smooth and sophisticated'.
- The use of similes to make descriptions more vivid and appealing, for example, 'as smooth as silk', 'as cool as a mountain stream'.
- The use of seemingly technical or scientific language, for example, 'a unique scientifically tested turbo-suction power motor'.
- **Puns** that play on the double meanings of words.

as cool as a mountain stream

How to Analyse an Advert

When analysing an advert and the effect that it creates you should look at four key points:

1. The heading / slogan – these are usually (but not always) in bigger print, so they stand out. Think about the effects and tone that the heading / slogan creates.
2. The use of photos / pictures / designs / illustrations, etc. Think carefully about the visual effects that are created.
3. The details given in the text – this is sometime called the 'blurb' and is usually in smaller print. What features and techniques have been used?
4. The overall effect that the advert has on you. What effect do all the individual parts create when put together in the advert?

Don't forget that not all adverts are effective so think about both the strengths and weaknesses.

Analysing an Advert

Look at this Magnum ice cream advertisement and study the techniques used in it.

💡 *Think about your overall response to the advert. Does it make you want to buy the ice cream?*

Note the catchy slogan: 'Enjoy the Royal Treatment'.

The gold pattern and 'M' crest set against a burgundy background give a feeling of richness and royalty.

Striking images of the ice cream surrounded by gold scrolls and topped with crowns give an instant sense of richness and luxury.

'Temptation' appears in large print, which draws attention to the ice cream's name. It also gives the impression of something that's a little bit naughty and indulgent.

'New' gives an impression of something new and exciting.

Adjectives are used to create effect – 'smooth', 'rich', 'indulgent', 'delicious'.

Repetition of 'chocolate' and 'chocolatey' emphasises the nature of the product.

ENJOY THE ROYAL TREATMENT

THE NEW MAGNUM
TEMPTATION

Temptation Caramel and Almonds and Temptation Chocolate. Smooth ice cream, rich sauce and indulgent chocolatey pieces all encased in delicious Belgian chocolate.

MAGNUM
WORLD'S PLEASURE AUTHORITY
www.mymagnum.co.uk

Quick Test

1. What is the purpose of advertisements?
2. What is an imperative?
3. Why might repetition be used in an advertisement?
4. Why might adjectives be used in an advert?

Media Texts – Advertisements

Key Words Exercise

Solve the clues to find the key words and complete the crossword.

Across

1. You take these with a camera. (11)
4. A term for describing words. (8)
10. What it's for. (7)
11. Various techniques create different _____. (7)
12. Adverts often use visual _____. (6)
13. Different _____ are used to create effects. (10)
14. A catchy heading. (6)
15. Adverts are often designed to sell these. (8)

Down

1. A technique that plays on double meanings of words. (4)
2. Words used to describe nouns. (10)
3. Commands. (11)
5. A bit over the top. (12)
6. You see these every day. (14)
7. The purpose of adverts. (8)
8. Again and again and again. (10)
9. In order to be effective, adverts must _____ to us. (6)

Look at the advertisement and answer the following questions.

1 What product is this advert for?

2 Who do you think the advert is aimed at?

3 Explain what effect is created by the main slogan and the sub-heading.

4 Why is the design with 'aah! Wednesday' used?

5 Where does the name of the company appear?

6 What is the purpose of the smaller print at the bottom of the advertisement?

7 How effective do you think the advert is?

FORGET THE TV NEWS.

Listen to your family's news, over chicken pie and gravy.

aah! WEDNESDAY

Make the pledge at bisto.co.uk & pick up family rewards

Media Texts – Advertisements

Look through magazines, newspapers, or any other sources where adverts are printed and choose two that you find interesting for some reason.

You don't have to find them both effective, although it would be useful if you thought at least one of them worked well.

Analyse each of your adverts carefully. You should look at the following features:
* The effect created by the heading(s) / slogan(s) and sub-heading(s).
* If other text is used, think about what information is given and how language is used.
* The visual effect created by photos / pictures / designs / illustrations, etc.
* The overall effect that the adverts have on you. Make sure you comment on both strengths and weaknesses and give reasons for your views.

Extension Activity

Now try designing an advertisement of your own.

Your advert can advertise anything you want. Think carefully about how you are going to create your effects. Here are some points to think about:
* What is your slogan or heading going to be?
* Are you going to use images of any kind?
* What kind of text will you use? What will it say? (Remember, you shouldn't add too much text otherwise people will not read it.)
* What techniques are you going to use to catch your reader's attention and make your advert persuasive?

When you have finished your advert, write an explanation of why you designed it as you did and what effects you wanted to create.

Then present your advert to a partner and discuss his / her response to it.

Shakespeare's Language

This topic looks at...

- Shakespeare's use of antithesis and oxymoron
- the use of personification
- the effects of hyperbole
- the use of puns.

Language Techniques

Although plays combine both words and action, **language** is at the heart of all Shakespeare's plays. It is through the language that the whole effect of the **drama** is created.

In order to create his effects, Shakespeare uses different kinds of language **techniques** that work together to create the overall experience of the play for the audience.

Here are some of the techniques that he uses in his plays:

SCENE 1

ROMEO:

But soft, what light through yonder window breaks?
It is the east, and Juliet is the sun.
Arise fair sun and kill the envious moon,
Who is already sick and pale with grief
That thou her maid art far more fair than she.
Be not her maid since she is envious.
Her vestal livery is sick and green,
And none but fools wear it; cast it off.

Shakespeare's Language

Antithesis

Antithesis puts two opposing thoughts or ideas together. It's a technique used a lot by Shakespeare, but one that we also use in our own everyday speech.

For example, if you say 'I love the subject, but I hate doing the work', you're using antithesis.

One of the best-known examples of antithesis from a Shakespearean play is the opening line of Hamlet's famous **soliloquy**: 'To be, or not to be: that is the question.' (A soliloquy is a speech given by a character when they're alone on the stage.)

In this soliloquy, Shakespeare juxtaposes the opposite ideas of existing or not existing. (**Juxtaposition** is when one idea is put next to another, i.e. a contrasting idea.)

The quotes below show some more examples from Shakespeare's plays.

The following example is the witches' chant from *Macbeth*:

> Fair is foul, and foul is fair;
> Hover through the fog and filthy air.

In *Othello*, Othello accuses his wife Desdemona of being false to him:

> Heaven truly knows that thou art as false as hell.

Here Othello uses antithesis (heaven / hell and true / false) in the simile to stress how false he believes Desdemona to be.

Oxymoron

Oxymoron is a very similar technique to antithesis. It puts two opposing words or ideas together in order to make a striking phrase or expression. For example, in *Romeo and Juliet*, when Juliet says goodbye to Romeo she says:

> Good Night, Good night! Parting is such sweet sorrow,
> That I shall say good night till it be morrow.

Here Shakespeare creates an effective phrase to capture Juliet's joy in her love and the thought of seeing Romeo again, contrasted with the sorrow she feels at parting from him.

Personification

Another technique that Shakespeare often uses to add effect to his language is personification. This describes an object or idea as if it were a human with human thoughts and feelings.

For example in *Romeo and Juliet*, Romeo uses personification to describe the tomb that contains Juliet:

> Thou detestable maw, thou womb of death,
> Gorg'd with the dearest morsel of the earth,
> Thus I enforce thy rotten jaws to open,

💡 *How do you think the tomb is described here?*

'Maw' is an old word that means 'stomach' – so in this example Romeo is describing the tomb as if it's a living thing that has eaten Juliet ('the dearest morsel of the earth'). He also describes it as a 'womb' – again something that a living being has. He intends to force the being's jaws open to get to his love.

In the following example from *Macbeth*, Shakespeare describes the country of Scotland, which is suffering under Macbeth's rule, as if it were a living thing that could be physically injured and feel pain and weep.

> I think our country sinks beneath the yoke;
> It weeps, it bleeds, and each new day a gash
> Is added to her wounds.

💡 *Think about the effects created by the use of personification in these examples. How has it made the image of the tomb or the country more vivid in your mind?*

Hyperbole

Hyperbole is the exaggerated and extravagant use of language to create a special impact or effect.

In the following example Othello, having passed through a violent storm at sea, is reunited with his beloved Desdemona. Look at the extravagant language that he uses to describe the storm and express his joy at being with Desdemona again.

💡 *Do you notice any other technique used here too?*

> It gives me wonder great as my content
> To see you here before me. O my soul's joy!
> If after every tempest come such calms,
> May the winds blow till they have waken'd death!
> And let the labouring bark climb hills of seas
> Olympus-high and duck again as low
> As hell's from heaven! If it were now to die,
> 'Twere now to be most happy; for, I fear,
> My soul hath her content so absolute
> That not another comfort like to this
> Succeeds in unknown fate

As well as hyperbole you might also have noticed the use of antithesis (tempest / calm, hell / heaven).

Shakespeare's Language

Puns

Shakespeare's plays are full of **puns** because the Elizabethan audiences of the times loved them. A pun is a play on words in order to create a funny effect. Puns work by playing around with words that have a double meaning or that sound similar to another word that means something quite different to the first word.

Lots of Shakespeare's puns are still obvious (and funny) today. However, sometimes it's not always easy to spot the puns or appreciate how funny they must have been to an Elizabethan audience. There are two reasons for this:

- The language has changed and so the meaning of the pun isn't immediately obvious.
- The modern sense of humour isn't quite the same as it was in the sixteenth century.

So, sometimes you might need to work at a pun to see what it might have meant to Shakespeare's audience.

The following two examples are from *Romeo and Juliet*:

Here Romeo is love-sick and gloomy, and his friend Mercutio is trying to cheer him up.

Can you spot the words that are played with?

> Mercutio: You are a lover; borrow cupid's wings,
> And soar with them above a common bound.
> Romeo: I am too sore empierced with his shaft
> To soar with his light feathers.

This example plays on the idea of soar (to fly) and sore (something painful).

Even when fatally wounded in a sword fight, Mercutio makes a pun.

> Romeo: Courage, man. The hurt cannot be much.
> Mercutio: No, 'tis not so deep as a well, nor so wide as a church door; but 'tis enough, 'twill serve. Ask for me to-morrow, and you shall find me a grave man.

Notice here how the play is on the word 'grave', which means 'serious' and is also the place where a dead person is buried.

Quick Test

1. A play on words is called a

   _____.

2. Exaggerated language is called

   _____.

3. A soliloquy is a speech given when the speaker is _____ on the stage.

4. When one idea or word is placed beside a contrasting idea, it's called

   _____.

KEY WORDS
Make sure you understand these words before moving on!
- Language
- Drama
- Techniques
- Antithesis
- Soliloquy
- Juxtaposition
- Oxymoron
- Personification
- Hyperbole
- Exaggerated
- Extravagant
- Puns

Work out the key words from the clues below, then find them in the word search.

1. Hyperbole is the _____ and _____ use of language.

2. A play is a form of this.

3. When contrasting words or ideas are placed next to each other it is called _____.

4. Shakespeare uses different _____ to create effects in his plays.

5. Describing a thing or an idea as if it were a living person.

6. A speech given by a character when he / she is alone on the stage.

7. Exaggerated language.

8. A striking phrase that uses opposing ideas.

9. Shakespeare uses many different kinds of _____ techniques in his plays.

10. Plays on words.

11. Two opposite thoughts or ideas that are put together.

E	S	T	A	A	F	C	A	Y	V	K	S	J	J	P
X	O	L	E	N	N	B	T	A	S	J	H	U	T	E
T	L	A	P	C	D	T	R	A	H	G	D	X	S	R
R	I	N	H	P	H	L	I	T	E	N	R	T	E	S
A	L	G	Y	F	C	N	H	T	G	C	A	A	V	O
V	O	U	P	T	D	Q	I	K	H	V	M	P	L	N
A	Q	A	E	R	F	E	J	Q	H	E	A	O	M	I
G	U	G	R	I	G	W	F	P	U	L	S	S	O	F
A	Y	E	B	H	B	R	A	P	U	E	A	I	C	I
N	W	E	O	Q	J	Y	E	L	S	N	S	T	S	C
T	Y	S	L	X	K	J	T	E	T	L	S	I	K	A
Q	N	R	E	T	E	I	O	D	A	Y	D	O	L	T
D	I	E	U	O	X	Y	M	O	R	O	N	N	G	I
J	E	X	A	G	G	E	R	A	T	E	D	S	T	O
P	E	R	S	O	P	E	X	A	G	E	R	A	D	N

Shakespeare's Language

1 In *Romeo and Juliet,* Juliet (from the Capulet family) finds that Romeo is from the family of her family's enemies (the Montagues). Shakespeare uses antithesis to express Juliet's feelings.

Explain how antithesis is used here and the effect it creates.

> My only love, sprung from my only hate!
> Too early seen unknown, and known too late!
> Prodigious birth of love it is to me
> That I must love a loathed enemy.

2 At the beginning of the play Romeo is in love with a girl called Rosaline, but she doesn't feel the same about him. Oxymoron is used to express his feelings.

Explain how oxymoron is used here and the effect it creates.

> O brawling love! O loving hate! . . .
> O heavy lightness! serious vanity!
> Misshapen chaos of well-seeming forms!
> Feather of lead, bright smoke, cold fire, sick health!
> Still-waking sleep, that is not what it is!
> This love feel I, that feel no love in this.

3 Explain the following puns from various Shakespearean plays.

a) From *Henry IV Part 1:*

> Pistol: To England will I steal, and there I'll steal.

b) From *Hamlet.* Hamlet's father is dead and Hamlet's uncle, who he really dislikes, has taken over as King and has married Hamlet's mother.

> Claudius: But now, my cousin Hamlet, and my son,-
> Hamlet: [Aside]   A little more than kin, and less than kind.
> Claudius: How is it that the clouds still hang on you?
> Hamlet: Not so, my lord; I am too much i' the sun.

c) From *Othello.* Othello approaches the sleeping Desdemona holding a burning torch or candle. He intends to kill her.

> Othello: Put out the light, and then put out the light.

Choose a Shakespearean play that you have studied or that you know.

1. Find one or more examples of Shakespeare's use of either antithesis or oxymoron in your chosen play. Explain how these example(s) work and what effects are created.

2. Find one or more example(s) of the use of personification in your chosen play. Explain how these example(s) work and what effects are created.

3. Find one or more puns in the play and explain how they work.

4. Write a short essay on how Shakespeare uses language in the play and the effects it creates. You could focus on just one section or act of the play.

Extension Activity

We use oxymorons or antithesis in everyday speech. For example…
- ill health
- small crowd
- probably definite.

Work with a partner to make up some of your own examples of oxymorons or antithesis. For each one write a short explanation of the phrase.

Reading for Meaning

What is Covered in this Topic?

This topic looks at...
- reading texts
- making notes
- finding information.

Reading your Text

How you approach reading a text can depend on what your **purpose** is in reading it. For example, the way in which you read a novel that you're really enjoying is likely to be different to the way in which you read an encyclopaedia to look for a particular entry.

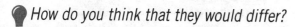 *How do you think that they would differ?*

You would probably read an enjoyable novel quite carefully at a reasonable, steady pace to take in all the details and enjoy the development of the characters and action, but in searching for a particular entry in an encyclopaedia you would probably cover a lot of text very quickly until you found the bit you wanted.

Remember, there are four different types of reading. The methods you will use depend on your purpose:

- **Skimming** – reading the text quickly and just 'skimming' it to get the main ideas. This can give you a quick overview of the text and also give you an idea of where certain points or pieces of **information** can be found.

- **Scanning** – a technique that you often use when you're looking for a particular piece of information. You will usually know what you're looking for to begin with and your initial scanning of the text might help to locate it quickly. It's also the kind of technique that you would use if looking for an entry in a telephone directory or a word in a dictionary.

- **Extensive reading** – this is the kind of reading you would probably use when reading a novel for pleasure, or a letter from a friend. It's the kind of reading you use when wanting to get a clear idea of what the text is saying.

- **Intensive reading** – this is a detailed reading to get an accurate idea of what the text says. You might use this to get a detailed understanding of a specific topic or to look closely at the way the language is used. For example, you might use this technique when analysing a poem or other piece of writing.

Making Notes

Making **notes** from books, magazines, the Internet and other sources can be very useful and even essential when preparing for activities such as writing an essay, sitting a test or producing a project of some kind.

Notes can remind you of things you've read, remind you of the key points, or help you to organise your revision.

Here are some points to think about when making your notes:

- Know why you're making your notes – what information are you looking for?
- Leave out anything that you don't need or which isn't relevant – sometimes notes are less useful because the note-maker hasn't been selective in the information they have included.
- Make sure that you note down the information accurately – inaccurate information will lead to mistakes in your work later.
- Use different note-making techniques to suit your purpose, e.g. bullet points, pattern notes or mind-maps.

Ugly appearance

Described as 'a loathsome reptile'

Character: FAGIN

Unpleasant character

Afraid of the gallows

Manipulates other characters

Cunning

Highlighting and Annotation

Depending on the kind of information you're making notes on, it can sometimes be useful (and quicker) to use **highlighting** and **annotation** on a copy of your text.

In this example, the student has highlighted the key ideas and jotted down brief notes to act as memory joggers when they look at the text again.

Macbeth is a tragedy by <u>William Shakespeare</u> about a <u>regicide</u> and its aftermath. It is Shakespeare's shortest tragedy and is believed to have been written some time between 1603 and 1606. The earliest account of a performance of the play is April 1611, when there is a record of such a play at the <u>Globe Theatre</u>.

→ Killing a king

Exact date uncertain →

Shakespeare's sources for the tragedy are the accounts of Kings <u>Macbeth</u>, Duff, and <u>Duncan</u> in <u>Holinshed's Chronicles</u> (1587), a history of England, Scotland and Ireland familiar to Shakespeare and his contemporaries.

← Idea for play

Others living at the same time as Shakespeare →

In the world of theatre, some actors believe the play is cursed and will not mention its name aloud, referring to it instead as <u>The Scottish play</u>.

← Some believe the play is cursed

Great actors have played the role →

Over the centuries, the play has attracted the greatest actors in the roles of Macbeth and Lady Macbeth. The play is still a favourite and is regularly performed on the stage and several film and television adaptations have been made.

← Film and TV versions made

Reading for Meaning

Comprehension

When you're asked to find specific information from a text you need to use your **comprehension** skills. This involves you understanding the text well. Before trying to answer any questions you should…

- read the text through at least once
- read the questions through carefully and make sure that you're clear what they're asking.

Remember to use skimming and scanning techniques to find the information you want and focus on certain points.

Writing a Summary

You might need to summarise the information in a text, either as part of your note-making or as part of a task that you've been set.

In order to write a **summary** you need to identify the **key points** in the text.

 Can you identify the key points in the passage below?

John Logie Baird and the invention of the television are part of History. But the idea of the television did not start with Logie Baird in the 1920s.

In the late nineteenth century, a number of scientists had made important discoveries that Baird would use in his first version of a television. Henri Becquerel found that light could be changed into electricity and, importantly, Ferdinand Braun had invented the cathode ray tube. By the 1920s there were 50 serious attempts to invent the television from Russia, America, Germany, Britain and Japan. Many researchers had well resourced and staffed laboratories but the man who invented the television did not.

John Logie Baird was born in 1888 near Glasgow. He had made money selling socks and soap. He sold off this business to follow his dream of inventing a television. It became an obsession and to survive he had to borrow money from friends and use whatever materials he could, including scraps.

By 1925, he was ready to give the first public display of a working television. The chosen place was Selfridges in Oxford Street, London. Shoppers saw slightly blurred but recognisable images of letters. In 1927, Baird demonstrated colour television and a video-recording system he called a 'Phonovision'. In 1928, Baird made the first transatlantic television transmission and one year later he started regular 30-line mechanical broadcasts.

In 1936, the BBC started the world's first regular high-definition service from Alexandra Palace using the Baird system, though it was abandoned one year later in favour of a system developed by Marconi-EMI. By 1939, 20,000 television sets were in use in Great Britain, just 14 years after Baird's first public demonstration of his system at work. In 1940, Baird gave a demonstration of a high-definition full colour stereo television.

Writing a Summary (cont.)

Here are some key points you might have noted:
- Television was invented by John Logie Baird.
- The actual idea of television began in the late nineteenth century.
- Many others attempted to invent television, often with well-equipped laboratories.
- Baird was born in 1888 near Glasgow and had little money or resources and had to borrow money to try to achieve his dream of inventing the television.

- In 1925, he gave the first public display of a working television in London.
- In 1927, Baird demonstrated colour television and a video-recording system.
- In 1928, he made the first transatlantic television transmission.
- In 1936, the BBC started the world's first television service using Baird's system.
- By 1939, 20,000 television sets were in use in Great Britain.

Quick Test

1. What's the first thing you need to be clear about when making notes?
2. What does annotation mean?
3. Comprehension means _____ your text.
4. When writing a summary you need to identify the _____ _____ in a text.

KEY WORDS
Make sure you understand these words before moving on!
- Purpose
- Skimming
- Information
- Scanning
- Extensive reading
- Intensive reading
- Notes
- Highlighting
- Annotation
- Comprehension
- Summary
- Key points

Reading for Meaning

Key Words Exercise

Complete each sentence by finding the missing key word.

1 Understanding a text involves using your _____ skills.

2 When reading a novel you probably use _____ _____ techniques.

3 A quick read just to get the main point of a text is called _____ .

4 Different reading techniques can help you find the _____ you're looking for in a text.

5 Making notes on a copy of your text is called _____ .

6 A _____ involves you identifying the key points from a text and writing a shortened version of it.

7 You can use _____ to mark the key words on a page and make them stand out.

8 _____ are an important way of recording ideas on what you read and can be an important tool for revision.

9 Detailed reading that you might use when analysing a text is called _____ _____ .

10 How you read a text depends on your _____ for reading it.

11 In writing a summary, you first need to identify the _____ _____ .

12 When looking for a number in a telephone directory you would use _____ techniques.

Read this extract, which is taken from _The Perfect Storm_ by Sebastian Junger, and answer the questions that follow.

Early fishing in Gloucester was the roughest sort of business, and one of the deadliest. As early as the 1650s, three-man crews were venturing up the coast for a week at a time in small open boats that had stones for ballast and unstayed masts. In a big wind the masts sometimes blew down. The men wore canvas hats coated with tar, leather aprons, and cowhide boots known as 'red jacks'. The eating was spare: for a week-long trip one Gloucester skipper recorded that he shipped four pounds of flour, five pounds of pork fat, seven pounds of sea biscuit, and 'a little New England rum'. The meals, such as they were, were eaten in the weather because there was no below-deck where the crews could take shelter. They had to take whatever God threw at them.

The first Gloucester fishing vessels worthy of the name were the thirty-foot chebaccos. They boasted two masts stepped well forward, a sharp stern, and cabins fore and aft. The bow rode the seas well, and the high stern kept out a following sea. Into the fo'c'sle were squeezed a couple of bunks and a brick fireplace where they smoked trashfish. That was for the crew to eat while at sea, cod being too valuable to waste on them. Each spring the chebaccos were scraped and caulked and tarred and sent out to the fishing grounds. Once there, the boats were anchored, and the men hand-lined over the side from the low midship rail. Each man had his spot called a 'berth', which was chosen by lottery and held throughout the trip. They fished two lines at twenty-five to sixty fathoms (150-360 feet) with a ten-pound lead weight, which they hauled up dozens of times a day. The shoulder muscles that resulted from a lifetime of such work made fishermen easily recognisable on the street. They were called 'hand-liners' and people got out of their way.

The captain fished his own lines, like everyone else, and pay was reckoned by how much fish each man caught. The tongues were cut out of the fish and kept in separate buckets; at the end of the day the skipper entered the numbers in a log book and dumped the tongues overboard. It took a couple of months for the ships to fill their holds – the fish was either dried or, later, kept on ice – and then they'd head back to port.

1 a) How many crew did the early boats have?
   b) What did they use for ballast?
   c) What sometimes happened to their masts?

2 Describe what the fishermen wore.

3 What do you think Junger means when he says 'The eating was spare'?

4 What were the first proper fishing boats called and how long were they?

5 Why do you think the fish the crew ate was called 'trashfish'?

6 What method of fishing do you think hand-lining is?

7 How were these fishermen easily recognisable on the street?

8 How were the fishermen paid?

9 Why were the tongues cut out of the fish they caught?

10 How were the fish preserved until the boat got back to port?

Reading for Meaning

Skills Practice

Select your own piece of writing. It can be a piece of fiction or non-fiction writing on any topic that you choose and should be about 350–400 words in length.

Write 8–10 questions on your piece of writing that you think would test someone's understanding of it.

Think carefully about the questions that you create and try to vary the style, e.g. some answers might be easily found in the passage but others might need working out from the things that have been said.

For each question that you create, ask yourself 'Could I answer this question if I had never seen the passage before?'

Questions

1.

2.

3.

4.

5.

6.

7.

8.

9.

10.

Extension Activity

Work with a partner and exchange your passages and questions.

Read each other's passages and try to answer each other's questions.

When you have finished, discuss these points:
- How easy or hard you found each other's questions.
- Any specific problems that you found in answering them.
- What kind of reading techniques you used in approaching the passage and the questions.

Make notes on the discussion and the key points made on both passages and sets of questions.

Punctuation

What is Covered in this Topic?

This topic looks at...
- contraction apostrophes
- commonly confused words
- possessive apostrophes.

The Apostrophe

There are two main reasons for using **apostrophes** in your writing:

1. To shorten a word or to combine two words together into one shortened form by missing out a letter or letters. Apostrophes used like this are called contraction apostrophes (or apostrophes of omission).

2. To show that someone owns something, i.e. to show **possession**. Apostrophes used like this are called **possessive** apostrophes.

These two reasons for using apostrophes are completely separate and you shouldn't muddle the two up.

Contraction Apostrophes

In some **contractions** two words are combined to create a new single unit. Note how an apostrophe replaces the dropped letters in each example:
- they're – they are (the 'a' is dropped)
- you've – you have (the 'h' and the 'a' are dropped)
- didn't – did not (the 'o' is dropped)

You'll be very familiar with these contractions and lots more like them. The mistake that is sometimes made, though, is to put the apostrophe where the two words join rather than where the letter(s) have been missed out.

For example:
- did'nt (✗)   didn't (✓)
- had'nt (✗)   hadn't (✓)

He didn't like flying

He hadn't got used to the noise

Punctuation

Sometimes contracted forms are confused with words that sound the same or are similar to other words. Words that sound the same but have different meanings are called homophones.

Here are some of the most commonly confused homophones:

Contracted form	Meaning	Homophone
It's	It is It has	Its (e.g. The dog lost *its* bone)
Who's	Who is	Whose (e.g. *Whose* bag is this?)
They're	They are	Their (e.g. *their* ball) or there (e.g. over *there*)
You're	You are	Your (e.g. *your* book)

💡 *Can you think of any other homophones that are created by contractions?*

You might have thought about the following that are often confused too:
- we're = 'we are', sometimes confused with...
  - were (e.g. We *were* going to the cinema)
  - wear (e.g. What are you going to *wear*?)
  - where (e.g. *Where* are you going?)
- here's = 'here is', sometimes confused with...
  - hears (e.g. He *hears* a sound.)

their ball

Possessive Apostrophes

Possessive apostrophes are probably more misused than any other punctuation mark:

1. Sometimes apostrophes are used when they should not be.
2. Sometimes an apostrophe is needed but is put in the wrong place.

Is An Apostrophe Needed?

The possessive apostrophe is used to show **ownership** or possession of something. For example:

The boy's book = The book belonging to the boy.

Apostrophes are never used on words that are simply plurals and are not indicating ownership. For example:

- The boy's went to town. (✗)
- The boys' went to town. (✗)
- The boys went to town. (✓)

If in doubt about whether or not an apostrophe is needed, ask yourself 'what belongs to the boy?' (as in this example). If you can't identify anything described as belonging to the boy then an apostrophe isn't needed.

Have a look at these sentences and see if you can identify those that need an apostrophe and those that don't.

- The mans hat was blown off.
- The girls pen fell on the floor.
- The trees bent with the force of the wind.
- The trees branch snapped off.

Here are the ones that needed an apostrophe:

- The man's hat was blown off.
- The girl's pen fell on the floor.
- The tree's branch snapped off.

Punctuation

Where Does the Apostrophe Go?

Once you've decided that an apostrophe is needed, the next question is 'where does it go?' There are two ways that you can work this out and if you use these checks, you should always get your apostrophes in the right place.

Method 1	Method 2
If the 'owner' is singular the apostrophe goes before the s ('s), e.g. 'The boy's house was in darkness'. (*one* boy) If the 'owner' is plural and the plural ends in s the apostrophe goes after the s (s'), e.g. 'The trees' roots were very deep'. (*more than one* tree) In cases like these where the plural ends in s the apostrophe actually tells you whether one boy or tree is meant or more than one. If the plural doesn't end in s then the apostrophe goes before the s ('s), e.g. 'The men's minibus broke down'. Here 'men' is the plural and doesn't end in s. In cases like this the actual word tells you that there is more than one man and so the apostrophe doesn't need to go after the s to show this.	Always put the apostrophe straight after the name of the 'owner'. For example: • The woman's bag (owner – the woman) • The women's party (owners – the women) • The cat's dish (owner – the cat – one cat) • The cats' bed (owner – the cats – more than one cat) Sometimes the ownership isn't clearly stated because the phrase is shortened, e.g. we often drop the word 'shop', 'house' and 'surgery' from phrases and use a shortened version such as butcher's meaning 'butcher's shop' or dentist's meaning 'dentist's surgery'. Watch out for these because these need apostrophes too, e.g. I'm going to the doctor's (doctor's surgery), I'll call at the baker's (baker's shop), I'm going round to Jim's (Jim's house).

Quick Test

Complete the sentences below.
1. Apostrophes that indicate ownership are called _____ apostrophes.
2. Shortened forms of words are called _____
3. Words that sound the same but have different meanings are called _____ .

Key Words Exercise

Unscramble these anagrams to discover the key words and then find the key words in the word search.

C	R	C	O	N	T	R	A	C	T	I	O	N	S	S	T
R	I	U	F	S	P	O	S	S	E	S	S	I	V	E	Q
K	D	E	L	H	B	O	B	I	T	F	B	Y	P	M	S
P	H	Y	G	H	O	O	W	L	D	D	B	P	V	P	J
O	A	E	H	S	R	M	Q	E	S	T	K	L	R	B	B
S	P	D	Y	Z	H	T	O	N	Y	K	J	U	I	B	U
S	A	P	O	S	T	R	O	P	H	E	S	R	O	Y	Z
E	A	B	J	G	M	M	G	B	H	R	M	A	W	T	J
S	I	K	T	J	N	E	S	L	C	O	N	L	N	N	H
S	E	D	T	B	O	A	I	B	O	U	N	Y	E	G	W
I	M	Y	L	C	D	N	N	U	N	V	H	E	R	T	L
O	W	X	P	E	Y	I	G	R	F	O	T	H	S	Z	R
N	B	M	M	H	Q	N	U	S	R	J	R	T	H	M	M
E	G	N	X	J	B	G	L	T	S	K	S	R	I	N	Q
L	A	C	X	J	B	S	A	R	T	D	U	S	P	V	H
R	Q	M	H	O	M	O	R	C	O	N	F	U	S	E	D

1. lapurl

2. whisperno

3. spiesnosos

4. raccoontints

5. snailrug

6. henhopmoos

7. focusend

8. evesissops

9. nameings

10. shapetroops

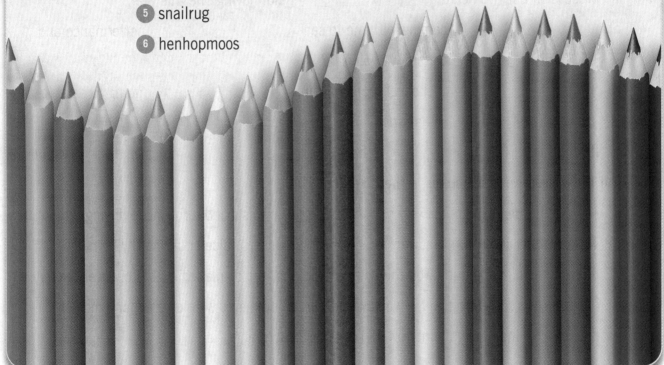

Punctuation

1 Complete the following sentences correctly using it's or its.

a) I know _____ raining and the forecast says _____ going to get worse.

b) The car has just had _____ annual service so, with a bit of luck, _____ going to get us to Cornwall without a problem.

c) The way that dog is baring _____ teeth and snarling, I think _____ going to turn nasty.

d) _____ always been an ambition of mine to become a film star but I don't think _____ going to happen.

e) The eagle swooped down onto _____ prey, grabbed it in _____ talons and flew back to _____ nest.

2 Complete these sentences using who's or whose; they're, their or there; your or you're.

a) _____ coming to stay this weekend and _____ bringing _____ nephew with them.

b) I went _____ last year and saw _____ carnival procession but I've heard _____ not having one this year.

c) _____ coming with me to see _____ performance and _____ car are we going in?

d) If _____ short of money again _____ going to have to use _____ savings.

e) If you've lost _____ book _____ not going to borrow mine.

3 Put the possessive apostrophes in these sentences.

a) The cars headlights were not very bright and the roads twists and turns made driving difficult.

b) The boys changing room was very noisy and the teachers voice could hardly be heard.

c) The young childs painting won the competition and was displayed in the towns art gallery.

d) The suns rays shone through the window and the old ladys eyes were dazzled for a moment.

e) I'm going to the doctors tomorrow so I'll get a prescription then.

Create a series of information sheets for Year 8 or Year 9 students explaining clearly how to use apostrophes correctly.

One information sheet should cover using contraction apostrophes.

One information sheet should cover commonly confused words.

One information sheet should cover using possessive apostrophes.

Try to make your information sheets informative, entertaining and eye-catching so think carefully about how you're going to design them. It would be useful, for example, to use illustrations to help present the information.

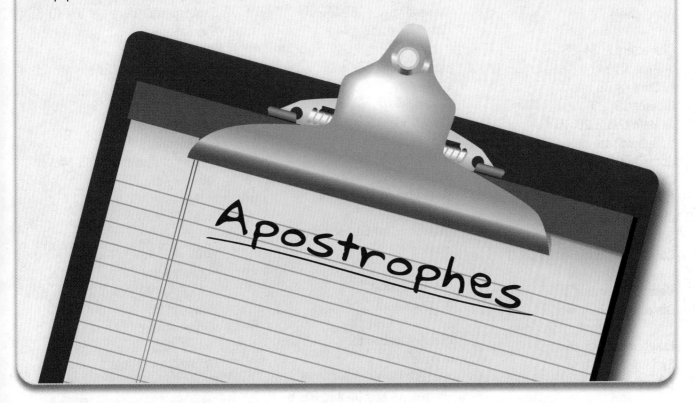

When you've finished your information sheets, create a worksheet to go with each information sheet in which you set questions or puzzles based on the use of apostrophes. Again, think about the design to try to make your worksheets as interesting as possible.

Work with a partner and exchange both information sheets and worksheets.

Read each other's worksheets carefully and make notes on...
- how easy to understand you found them
- how effective the presentation was
- any suggestions for improvement.

Try doing the work that your partner set on the worksheets and note how well you felt this work helped to reinforce how to use apostrophes.

Discuss your thoughts and ideas on each other's work.

Index

ACKNOWLEDGEMENTS

The authors and publisher are grateful to the copyright holders for permission to use quoted materials and images.

Page 7 *Coming up for Air* by George Orwell (Copyright©George Orwell) By permission of Bill Hamilton as the Literary Executor of the Estate of the Late Sonia Brownell Orwell and Secker & Warburg Ltd

Page 37 Extract from *Of Mice and Men* by John Steinbeck (Penguin, 2000). Copyright © John Steinbeck, 1937, 1965. Reproduced by permission of Penguin Books Ltd

Page 40 Leaflets supplied by West Yorkshire Police

Page 41 Leaflets supplied by West Yorkshire Police

Page 44 ©RSPCA Photolibrary

Page 47 `War Photographer` is taken from "*Standing Female Nude*" by Carol Ann Duffy published by Anvil Press Poetry in 1985

Page 51 'Blackberry-Picking' is taken from Death of a Naturalist © Seamus Heaney and reproduced by permission of Faber and Faber Ltd.

Page 54 Imtiaz Dharker, *Postcards from god* (Bloodaxe Books, 1997)

Page 55 *Green Days by the River* by Michael Anthony, reproduced by permission of Carlton Publishing Group

Page 58 *Be a Butterfly* by Grace Nichols, reproduced by permission of Curtis Brown Group Ltd ©1984

Page 63 Magnum Temptations Advertisement reproduced with kind permission of Unilever

Page 65 ©Premier Foods

Page 76 ©Chris Trueman

Page 79 Copyright © 1997 by Sebastian Junger. Reprinted with permission of the Stuart Krichevsky Literary Agency, Inc.

P.4   ©iStockphoto.com / Joachim Angeltun
P.11 ©iStockphoto.com / Kim Freitas
P.17 ©iStockphoto.com / Joan Loitz
P.22 ©iStockphoto.com / Rodrigo Eustachio
P.27 ©iStockphoto.com / Justin Welzien
P.32 ©iStockphoto.com / Kim Bryant
P.45 ©iStockphoto.com / Julien Grondin
P.52 ©iStockphoto.com / Kim Freitas
P.60 ©iStockphoto.com / Kim Freitas

All other images ©2009 Jupiterimages Corporation, and Lonsdale.